NIGERIAN CONSTITUTIONAL LAW

Selected Issues

NIGERIAN CONSTITUTIONAL LAW
Selected Issues

Aboaba O. Omotesho

malthouse MP

Malthouse Press Limited

Lagos, Benin, Ibadan, Jos, Port-Harcourt, Zaria

This Edition 2024
ISBN 978-978-60618-8-7

Published by Malthouse Press Limited

Lagos Port Harcourt Zaria

43 Onitana Street, Off Stadium Hotel Road,
Off Western Avenue, Lagos Mainland
E-mail: malthouselagos@gmail.com
Facebook:@malthouselagos
Twitter:@malthouselagos
Instagram:@malthouselagos
Tel: 0802 600 3203

International Distributors
African Books Collective, Oxford, UK
Email: abc@africanbookscollective.com
Website: http://www.africanbookscollective.com

FOREWORD

After nearly 30 long and disastrous years of military rule in Nigeria from 1966 to 1999 (less only four wobbly years of civilian interregnum from 1979 to 1983), the culture of constitutionalism in the country has become brutally defaced, degraded and obscured. The return of constitutional government in May 1999 marked a new beginning for virtually everybody – the politicians, the legislators, the students, the academia and all. No wonder that all levels of government – Federal, State and Local Government – the nation has been experiencing a rattling bustle of inter-governmental disputation as to the limits of power and the dos and don'ts of governmental action.

Under these circumstances, it is happy to welcome this collection of essays written by my young colleague A.O. Omotesho. Appropriately titled, *Nigerian Constitutional Law, Selected Issues*, the author in ten short essays covered the main issues of constitutional law, which are relevant and topical in the present Nigerian situation. Each chapter of the book is devoted to a particular issue and discusses it in simple, straightforward and analytical style. In this way, the essays are inviting to read and are free from the tedium usually associated with complicated and theoretically abstracted research.

The essays are written primarily for University law students and students in other tertiary institutions studying constitutional law either as a core course or as a required ancillary course. The book thus serves an important need to make academic materials available to such students in these days of harrowing book scarcity in the country. But the essays will also reward reading by politicians and others, including lawyers, who may want or need to read up elements of constitutional law or to brighten their dimming knowledge of rudiments of the subject.

The author makes no claim or pretension to details or exhaustiveness in their treatment of the issues discussed. Any good student therefore committed to excellence will need to consult additional materials. For this reason, the author has been concerned to provide at the end of each chapter a list of references for further reading.

Finally, I want to put on record my deep appreciation for this effort by A. O. Omotesho and commend the book for gainful reading by those to whom it is addressed.

CHARLES ILEGBUNE
Professor of Law, University of Abuja.

ABBREVIATIONS AND ACRONYMS

AFRC	Armed Forces Ruling Council
AJC	Advisory Judicial Committee
AU	African Union
CJN	Chief Justice of Nigeria
COP	Commissioner of Police
CPC	Criminal Procedure Code
ECOWAS	Economic Organisation of West African States
FCT	Federal Capital Territory
FEC	Federal Executive Council
FMG	Federal Military Government
ING	Interim National Government
JSC	Justice of the Supreme Court
NASS	National Assembly
NBA	Nigerian Bar Association
NCS	National Council of States
PRC	Provisional Ruling Council
SMC	Supreme Military Council
UNO	United Nations Organisation
UNGA	United Nations General Assembly

CASES

Lahan v. Attorney General Western Region (1962) WNLR 319; 119

Lakanmi *v.* Att. General Western State (1971) 1 UILR 201; 114

Lawal Kagoma *v.* Gov. Kaduna State (1982) 3 NCLR 1032; 89

Liverseige v. Anderson (1942) AC 206; 75

Marbury v. Madison 1 CR 137 (1803); 21, 100

Mcculloch *v.* Maryland 4 Wheat 316 (1819); 83

Merchant Bank *v.* Fed. Minister of Finance (1961) 1 All NLR 598; 63

Magaji *v.* Board of Customs & Excise (1982) NCLR 552

Momoh v. Okewale (1977) 6 SC 81; 124

Momoh v. Senate (1981) 1 NCLR p.21; 22

Obarioge v. Governor of Ondo State (1982) 3 NCLR 349; 63

Obiefuna v. Okoye (1961) All NLR 357; 123

Ojukwu v. Lagos State Govt (1985), 2 NWLR part 10 p. 806; 18

Ojukwu *v.* Lagos State Govt (1986) 1 NWLR (pt 18) 621; 23

Okogie *v.* Att. General Lagos State (1982) 2 NCLR 218; 46, 68, 73

Okpaku v. Resident Plateau Province (1985) N. N. L. R. 5; 76

Okwu *v.* Wayas (1981) 2 NCLR p.522; 24

Onye *v.* Anegbudu (1983) NCLR 492; 65

Olawoyin *v.* C.O.P (1961) 2 All NLR 203; 102

Orisakwe v. Gov of Imo State (1980) 3 NCLR 743; 63

Orisakwe *v.* Gov of Imo State (1982) 3 NCLR 743; 18

Oyegbami *v.* Att. General Federation (1982) 3 NCLR 895; 67

R *v.* Amalgamated Press Ltd (1961) All NLR 199; 68

R *v.* Comm. For Lagos Ex parte Cherubim & Seraphim (1960) LLR 123; 75

R. *v.* Electricity Commissioner (1965) NMLR 295; 76

STATUTES

- ✓ 31; 51
- ✓ 32; 52
- ✓ 33-38; 71
- ✓ 33; 56-58
- ✓ 33(1); 57
- ✓ 33(2); 57, 58
- ✓ 34; 56, 58
- ✓ 34(1); 59
- ✓ 35; 56
- ✓ 35(1); 60
- ✓ 35(2); 62
- ✓ 36; 56, 62
- ✓ 36(1); 62, 63
- ✓ 36(2); 62
- ✓ 36(3); 62
- ✓ 36(4); 63
- ✓ 36(5)-(12); 63
- ✓ 37; 56, 63
- ✓ 37-41; 71
- ✓ 38; 56, 65
- ✓ 39; 56, 67
- ✓ 39(1); 65, 66
- ✓ 39(2); 65, 66
- ✓ 39(3); 65
- ✓ 40; 56, 40, 68, 69
- ✓ 41; 66, 69
- ✓ 41(1); 69
- ✓ 41(2); 58, 69
- ✓ 42; 56
- ✓ 42(1); 70

- ✓ 42(2); 70
- ✓ 42(3); 70
- ✓ 43; 56, 70
- ✓ 43(2)(f); 71
- ✓ 45; 56, 66, 71
- ✓ 45(1); 64, 71
- ✓ 45(2); 62, 71
- ✓ 45(3); 71
- ✓ 46; 56, 72, 101
- ✓ 46(1); 72, 73
- ✓ 46(2); 73
- ✓ 46(3); 73
- ✓ 46(4); 73
- ✓ 84; 108
- ✓ 122-161; 37
- ✓ 124; 108
- ✓ 143; 91
- ✓ 143(3); 96
- ✓ 147(2); 90
- ✓ 147(4); 91
- ✓ 155; 90
- ✓ 160(2); 95
- ✓ 162-172; 37
- ✓ 174; 89
- ✓ 174(1); 95
- ✓ 175(1); 94
- ✓ 175(2); 95
- ✓ 188; 91
- ✓ 192(2); 90
- ✓ 211(1); 95

FOREIGN

GHANA

FRANCE

UK

USA

INTERNATIONAL

CONTENTS

3: HISTORICAL DEVELOPMENT OF NIGERIAN CONSTITUTIONAL LAW

4: FUNDAMENTAL OBJECTIVES AND CONCEPT OF CITIZENSHIP UNDER NIGERIAN CONSTITUTION

5: REFLECTIONS ON THE NATURE OF FUNDAMENTAL RIGHTS

6: LEGISLATIVE POWERS UNDER NIGERIAN CONSTITUTION

7: SCOPE OF EXECUTIVE POWERS UNDER NIGERIAN CONSTITUTION

8: JUDICIAL POWERS AND CONCEPT OF JUDICIAL INDEPENDENCE UNDER NIGERIAN CONSTITUTION

Chapter 1

DEFINITIONS AND FORMS OF CONSTITUTIONAL LAW

The word "Constitution" has been variously defined by writers and authors of the subject. Thus, like most concepts the word constitution, defies a single definition owing to the different perceptions of it.

In the perception of Hood Phillips,[1] the word Constitution is used in two different senses the abstract and the concrete sense. In the abstract sense, he said, it is the system of laws, customs and conventions which define the composition and powers of organs of the state, and regulate the relations of the various state organs to one another and to the private citizen.

The author defined a constitution in its concrete sense as the document in which the most important laws of the constitution are authoritatively ordained.

The definition by Hood Phillips in the abstract sense raises no problem as it appears to be in line with the consensus of most writers or authors of Constitutional law that a constitution seeks to set out the structure and working of the various organs of government as obtained in any given community. The other definition raises the problem of

---

[1] O. Hood Philips and Paul Jackson, *Constitutional and Administrative Law*, 6th edn. (1978 Sweet & Maxwell) P. 15

interpretation. If it is interpreted to mean a single document, then it is not all nations of the world that have a Constitution in the form of a single document. In the case of Britain which does not have it embodied in a single document, the definition could embrace it in the sense of the various constitutional documents which can be referred to as important laws that are authoritatively ordained.

According to Oluyede[2] it is an expression, whether in documentary form or unwritten, of legal principles, rules, laws and in some cases, conventions or customs in accordance with which a country is governed and by which its citizens are bound.

One cannot but agree with the general consensus of writers that a constitution is that supreme law of the land, which defines the structure of the organs of state and the relationship between these organs with one another on the one hand and with citizens of the state on the other hand.

RATIONALE FOR A CONSTITUTION

The question that may be asked is: why is it necessary to have a Constitution? The answers are not far-fetched. Generally speaking, a constitutional government defines the scope of the exercise of state powers by those in authority. A constitutional government is predicated upon the notion that governance must be conducted in accordance with the dictates of the law which is a product of the people with whom power lies or by their representatives. Thus, a constitution is desirable for the following reasons:

---

[2] P.A.O. Oluyede, *Constitutional Law in Nigerian*, 1st edn (Evans Brothers; 1992) Page 1

1. to specify the powers of state organs to avoid arbitrariness, e.g., the specification of executive powers, legislative powers and judicial powers;
2. ensure accountability of those vested with power to the governed e.g. appropriation of fund;
3. protection of minorities against the majority rule and need to ensure equality of all, e.g., right to freedom from discrimination;
4. desire to secure and protect fundamental rights and freedom from state power, e.g., right to freedom of expression;
5. the need or desire to be guided by certain cherished ideals which must be attained for the betterment of the society, e.g. the Fundamental Objectives and Directive Principles of State Policy;
6. the desire to break up with the past owing to liberation from colonial rule or because of a war or revolution, e.g., The 1960 Constitution; the 1787 American Constitution came into being after the American War of Independence.

The achievement of these goals or desire is the collective responsibility of all the people who have firmly resolved to have the constitution and must do all that is necessary towards its realization. In this regard, it is pertinent for the Constitution to be Supreme and ensure that it is binding on every authority.

SOURCES OF CONSTITUTION

The sources of Constitutions can be seen as the material evidence from which a constitutional lawyer derives a source of rule on a given subject. Broadly speaking, a Constitution of any country of the world is either written or unwritten. The sources sometimes depend on whether it is written or unwritten constitution, although as we shall see, they have somewhat become flexible and applicable to both.

Statutes or legislations

Statutes or legislations constitute the bulk of the sources and therefore be regarded as a Primary source of Constitution. Examples are: the 1999 Nigerian Constitution; the 1787 United States Constitution; the Constitution of the Federal Republic of Germany; etc. Apparently this source is in line with written constitutions. But even in some cases of unwritten constitutions, there are evidences of some historical documents from which the British Constitution can be gleaned. The British Constitution is regarded as one of the best examples of an Unwritten Constitution. Since there is no book referred to as the Constitution of Great Britain, but there are series of Parliamentary Acts (Legislation) that are Constitutional in nature. Examples are the Petition of Rights, 1628, The Bill of Rights, 1689, The Act of Union of Scotland, 1908, The Parliament Act, 1911 and the Judicature Act, 1925 etc. All these and other such statues form a veritable source of unwritten constitution of Great Britain.

Judge-made Law (Case Law) or Precedents)

Judge-made Law (Case Law) or Precedents) is also another primary source of constitution and also cuts across and applicable to both written and unwritten constitutions. The doctrine of Judicial Precedent applies to constitutional law as well as other branches of law. It is to the effect that a decision of a superior court is binding on inferior or lower courts faced with similar facts and circumstances. Such interpretation of statues by judges or constitutional matters therefore becomes a binding rule on others and consequently a source of law.

Conventions

Conventions are rules based on customs and practices that have evolved over a long period of time. A.V. Dicey defines conventions as rules for determining the mode in which the discretionary powers of the Crown ought to be exercised[3] Expanding on this definition, an author says they represent some understanding, tacitly agreed upon and based on a long practice by which the conduct of the crown, parliament and cabinet was regulated in cases where there were no rules.[4]

Thus, a convention is any binding rule of behaviour accepted as obligatory by those to whom it applies. However, a convention must be clearly distinguishable from a legal rule. For a rule to qualify as a convention, it must be accepted as a binding rule and it is only applicable in the absence of a legal rule on the subject. Conventions constitute a quick source of unwritten constitution, e.g. Britain where the appointment and removal of Prime Minister, the selection of cabinet ministers, etc., all rest upon convention. As for written constitutions, conventions have no place, but, many conventions have been embodied in written constitutions especially in Commonwealth countries. It is important to point out that even though conventional rules have no force of law, a breach of it will eventually lead to a breach of law.

---

[3] A.V. Dicey, *Introduction to the study of the Law of the Constitution*, 10th edition, 1959, Chapters 14 and 15

[4] Aihe, D.O. *Selected Essays on Nigerian Constitutional Law*, (1979) Ibadan Press Limited P.1

The **Common Law**

The Common Law, which has its origin from Britain and which has been received and applied in many countries of the world, is also a rich source of constitution especially in the Commonwealth countries or other English-speaking nations. In this regard, mention must be made of the principles of equity which developed subsequently to supplement some of the rigid principles of common law. Thus, Common Law and equitable principles which are constitutional in nature are also important in considering the sources of constitution.

Literature

Literature - which consists of writings of jurists, political thinkers, philosophers, statesmen and other landmark contributions on constitutional issues - constitutes a vital source of constitution especially on constitutional practices and procedures.

FORMS OF CONSTITUTION

The classification of constitution is intended to categorize constitutions according to certain objects or purpose, which they serve, or certain characteristics they possess for realization of certain objectives.

Conventionally, constitutions are classified into written and unwritten, rigid and flexible, supreme and non-supreme, federal and parliamentary, unitary and presidential, and each of these will be examined in turn.

(a) Written and Unwritten

This classification is said to be very illogical, outdated and unhelpful. It does not seem to serve any useful purpose because there is no country in the world that has no constitution which is wholly written and wholly unwritten.

Britain is, often cited as the sole surviving example of a country with a constitution that is unwritten. The truth however, is that there are various Acts of the British parliament which are of constitutional nature. Examples of these are:

- Magna Carta of 1215;
- Petition of Rights of 1628;
- Bill of Rights of 1689;
- Act of Settlement of 1700;
- Acts of Parliament, 1911;
- Judicature Act of 1925, etc.

The British Constitution is therefore not a written constitution in the sense that the rules of the constitutional law of that country are not embodied in a single document and also because most of the English constitutional rules derive from conventions and usages which are indeed more important than some of the written constitutional rules.

Even where a country has the legal rules of the constitution embodied in one single document, these rules are either supplemented or modified or departed from by constitutional conventions, usages, and practices. Therefore, such constitutions though written in a single document, do not consist of only written legal rules. Indeed, where constitutional conventions have developed, some of them may be more important than the written rules of the constitution.

It is as a result of the foregoing therefore, that it is said that this mode of classification does not serve any value; as it does not advance our understanding of different constitutions and their distinctive features.

(b) Rigid and Flexible

This classification owes its origin to Lord Bryce in his book, *Studies in History and Jurisprudence.* According to the jurist, a constitution is rigid when for its formal amendment; a special procedure or machinery is provided. Where the legal process for amendment is the same as that for making ordinary laws, a constitution is described as flexible.

Based on this distinction, most of the constitutions of the world barring New Zealand, England and the defunct USSR can be categorised as rigid constitutions. Interestingly, a constitution, which is rigid in outlook, may indeed be quite flexible to amend. Conversely, a constitution, which is flexible theoretically, may actually be rigid to amend in practice. A typical illustration of the latter is the third Republic Constitution of France. That constitution in theory is flexible in that it required only a simple majority of both houses of the national assembly at a joint sitting for its amendment. However, since both houses were never in agreement, any bill emanating from either of the houses can be rejected by the other.

Rigidity of the constitution varies from constitution to constitution. Where a special, procedure is prescribed, it may be in respect of the voting procedure or it may also be in respect of the bodies that may be associated with the amendment procedure.

Generally, where a special procedure is prescribed, it is either the legislature sitting separately or in joint session. Where special machinery is prescribed, it may be the ordinary legislature making the amendment in association with other bodies. For example, the 1999 constitution of Nigeria can be amended by two-thirds (⅔) of states. In the case of amendment of the fundamental rights provision and the amending provision itself, as well as the provision dealing with creation of states, the National Assembly requires four-fifth (⅘) majority in both Houses.

The Australian and New Zealand constitutions are the examples of those constitutions where the legislature alone cannot amend the constitution. The approval of the people in referendum is a further requirement.

Not, however, that the fact that a constitution is rigid in outlook should not lead one to conclude that such a constitution is difficult to amend in practice. The rigidity of the constitution in practice would depend upon a variety of factors such as:

i. whether the constitution is accepted to the most powerful group in the country;
ii. whether the minorities whose rights are protected by the constitution would regard a particular amendment as posing danger to their interests;
iii. where the constitution is the enactment of a foreign power, it may not be acceptable to the people of the country either because of its unsuitability or its variance with the character, attitude and culture of the citizenry. Invariably, such people will seize the first opportunity to tamper with the constitution.

Even when the constitution is rigid in theory, the people working the constitution may be so dynamic in their approach and as such they would keep experimenting with constitution so as to serve their national interest, the higher values and objectives which the people cherish most. For example, the constitution of Switzerland, which is regarded as the most rigid in outlook, has been subjected to frequent amendments because of the adaptability of the people of that country to new situations.

The Austrian constitution, which contains similar amending provisions, has only been subjected to amendment half a dozen times. Therefore, in classifying the constitution into rigid and flexible categories, one should have regard to the suitability of the particular constitution for that country.

Remarkably, a constitution even if rigid in theory, may in practice be flexible if the group in power finds it convenient in the pursuit of that group's perpetuation in power. On the other hand, where a constitution is flexible, as in the case of New Zealand, its amendment may be highly difficult. This may be the consequence of the political consciousness of the people. Thus, the legislature is compelled to first ascertain public opinion on any proposed amendment before actually embarking upon amending the constitution.

Even where the ordinary law-making procedure may amend the constitution, the members of the legislature may indeed, react quite differently when considering the amendment of the constitution.

The foregoing are the external factors that ascribe rigidity to an otherwise flexible constitution.

(c) Supreme and Non-Supreme

A constitution is said to be supreme when the provisions are binding upon every authority established under the constitution including the legislature. The supremacy of a constitution depends upon the extent to which limitation imposed thereby can be enforced in a legal manner.

Where a constitution stipulates the procedure to be adopted in passing a law by the legislature, it is argued that it is not the constitution but the legislature that is supreme. This is because ultimately, it is the legislature that passes the law. It is also contended that any special procedure contained in the constitution does not limit the powers of the legislature and that once the legislature passes a law even without following the special procedure, it is law because the legislature has declared it so.

The Supreme Court of South African in HARRIS v. DANGES and the Privy Council in the Ceylonese case of bribery, COMMISSIONER v. RANSINGE, took the view that when the constitution prescribes the form and manner to be followed by the legislature in making a law including a constitutional amendment, the courts reserved the power, to inquire into the question whether the law made by the legislature is in accordance with the formal manner, so prescribed; Where the formal manner so prescribed is not followed, the action of the legislature will be unconstitutional.

In such cases, although the legislature actually passes the law, the formal manner prescribed in the constitution, serves as control on the legislature and therefore to that extent, it is the constitution and not the legislature that is supreme and sovereign.

Note that a constitution, which is rigid, is invariably a supreme constitution because for amending the constitution, the legislature has to follow the special procedure. Note also that a federal constitution must also be supreme. For examples section 1(i) of the 1999 Constitution of Nigeria provides that:

> This constitution is supreme and its provisions shall have binding force on all authorities through the Federal Republic of Nigeria.

(d) Federal and Unitary

In both the Federal and Unitary constitutions, there exists two levels of government but the distinction between them lies in the manner in which the federal or central government relates to the regional or state government.

A constitution is said to be federal in nature when the two levels of governments are constituted for different purposes such that each exercises powers given to it by the constitution in a manner independent and in co-ordination with the other level of government. The relationship between the federal legislature and the state legislature is that of a coordinate and not one of subordination.

In a federal constitution, there is a division of powers between the central and state government such that the central government is constituted for certain purposes. The government can only exercise those powers conferred on it by the constitution. In exercising their respective powers, both levels of government function independently of each other. The exercise of power by one is not subject to control or approval of the other.

A constitution is unitary in form when the entire power by law is vested in the central government and the units are created or constituted by the law made by the central legislature. Under a unitary constitution, the powers of the states or units are derived from the central government subject to such conditions as may be imposed by the central government. The existence of the states also depends upon the central government. The exercise of the powers by the state government may also be subjected to approval or supervision by the central authority. Thus, in a unitary constitution, there may be two levels of governments exercising different powers. However, the position of the unit the central government is that of a subordinate.

According to this classification, the constitutions of America, Canada, Australia, Switzerland, India and Nigeria may be regarded as federal. The constitutions of New Zealand, France and Irish Republic are examples of unitary constitution.

(e) Parliamentary and Presidential

This classification is based upon whether a constitution has incorporated the doctrine of separation of powers. By separation of powers, we mean that the power of the state is divided between the legislature, Executive and Judiciary. But for the purpose of classification of constitutions, we are mostly concerned with the division of powers between the Executive and Legislature.

In a parliamentary type of government, the executive is a part of the legislature. Ministers who exercise executive powers, wholly consists of the members of the legislature who sit, take part in proceedings of the legislature and being answerable to the legislature, hold their office only so long as they have the confidence or support of the legislature. If they forfeit the legislative confidence, the council of ministers has simply to go.

The entire legislative business is planned and initiated by the council of ministers. When they have an absolute majority in their support by the use of party whip and the threat of dissolution of the legislature, they can control the legislature to approve any legislation they initiate. The executive under this system of government may also get the law making power delegated to it to any extent the legislature may decide.

Under presidential types of constitution, there is a clear separation of powers between the executive and legislature in that both are directly elected by the people and hold their office for a fixed period of time.

The executives are answerable to the people and not to the legislature. The legislature too is not subject to the dissolution power of the executives. Although under checks and balances, the executive has been subjected to the control of the legislature under the impeachment process, which the latter can exercise upon specified grounds.

The executive is not part of the legislature nor can they sit or take part in the proceedings of the legislature. The executive may however, send draft bills proposing new legislation to the legislature, which may or may not be acted upon.

Although the law making power is vested in the legislature, in practice it has become necessary to delegate subordinate and constitutional law making power to the executives. This practice, the courts had to accept as constitutionally permissible.

REFERENCES FOR FURTHER READING

O'Hood Philips & Paul Jackson, *Constitutional Law & Administrative Law*, 6th edition.

Oluyede, P.A.O., *Constitutional Law in Nigeria*, Evans Brothers

Aihe, D.O. (1979), *Selected Essays on Nigerian Constitutional Law*

Dicey, A.V. (1959), *Introduction to the study of the Law of the Constitution*, 6th edition

Chapter 2

COMMON CONSTITUTIONAL CONCEPTS

The enormous coercive power which the state possesses is capable of being exercised to oppress and deny the liberties and freedoms of the individuals. Hence, for centuries the discussion on how to control and regulate the exercise of this power has been going on and still the question has not been satisfactorily resolved. The necessity to control and restrict the absolute power of the state over the individual led to the formation of constitutional theories and movements. The movement resulted in the establishment of constitutional governments whose authority was limited by the terms of the constitution. The limitations on governmental power and the extent of such limitation did not follow any uniform pattern. The experiences materially vary from one place to another.

RULE OF LAW

The greatest protagonist of the concept of the Rule of Law is Professor A.V. Dicey. His formulation of the concept thought criticized over the years has however remained the most comprehensive analysis ever attempted. A.V. Dicey approach the concept of Rule of Law from three angles.

a. That the Rule of Law signifies the supremacy of law over arbitrary use of power. According to him "*English men* *are ruled by law alone but cannot be punished for something else."* In effect this first perspective connotes the exercise of power in accordance with ordinary law of the land. For example in AGBAJE v. COMMISSIONER OF POLICE[1] the applicant was ordered to be detained by the Inspector General of Police under Section 3(1) of the Armed Forces and Police (Special Powers) Decree no 24 of 1967. The Commissioner of Police in carrying out the orders of the I.G.P detained the applicant at a police station instead of Prison custody as directed. It was held that such detention in police custody was invalid being contrary to the law under which the Commissioner purported to be acting. In the case ESHUGAYI ELEKO v. THE GOVERNMENT OF NIGERIA[2] the colonial government claimed an inherent power to appoint and depose as well as report traditional chiefs in pursuance of which the applicant was first restricted and upon his refusal to comply was deported. The court held that the government could only act under express power conferred on it for this purpose by law. The court held further that the British jurisprudence recognized that no member of the executive can interfere with the liberty or property of a British subject except on the condition that the legality of the action can be supported in an action before the court of justice.

In RE MOHAMMED OLAYORI & ORS[3] the applicant were at the material time contractors to the Nigerian Army. They were alleged to have received money from the Army for services not rendered or goods not supplied. They were consequently detained purportedly on the orders of the Chief

---

[1] SUIT NO. CAW/81/69
[2] (1931) AC 662
[3] SUIT No M/196/69

of Staff Supreme Headquarters who was allegedly exercising his powers under Section 3 of the Armed Forces and Police (Special Powers) Decree 1967. The court held that the detention of the applicants was illegal based as it were on no legal authority. The submission of the state counsel to the effect that the Chief of Staff had unlimited powers to order detention of any person under the Decree according to his discretion caused the learned trial judge J.I.C Taylor to make the following observations:

> If we are to live by the Rule of Law and if we are to have our actions guided and restrained in certain ways for the benefit of the society in general and individual members in particular, then whatever status, whatever post we hold, we must succumb to the Rule of Law. The alternative anarchy and chaos.

b. The second aspect of rule of law according to Dicey is that all men are equal before the law or "the equal subjection of all classes to the ordinary law of the land administered by the ordinary court". In this sense, all officials no matter how highly placed must obey the law which governs the ordinary citizens. To dramatize the essence of this second formulation of Rule of Law, one may advert to a conversation that took place between King James I of England and Lord Justice Coke as far back as the Seventeenth Century. The King told Justice Coke:

> "*then I am under the law, it is treason to affirm it.*"
> Coke replied: "*... the King is under no man but under God and the law.*"

The Supreme Court of the United States of America applied this principle during the Watergate crisis involving President Nixon. The President has committed what was perceived a crime by authorizing the breaking into the headquarters of the opposing Democratic Party. Nixon also received all transactions in the oval house on tape. The conversations authorizing the breaking into the democratic office was also on tape. The President refused to release the tapes on grounds of presidential immunity. The American Supreme Court ordered the release of tape and President Nixon lost his office as a result of the subsequent revelations.

The case of OJUKWU v. LAGOS STATE GOVERNMENT[4] further illustrates the issue of executive obedience to the rule of law in that case the Court of Appeal declared null and void the action of Lagos State Government in physically dislodging the appellant from his residence without first obtaining an order of court as provided for under the recovery of premises law of Lagos State.

In BELLO v. SANNI[5] the plaintiff was appointed Auditor General before 1979 Constitution came into being. He was deemed to retain the position. However, the Governor of Kaduna State purported to remove him from that position on filing the suit in court challenging the removal, it was held that under Section 119 of the Constitution, the Governor could only remove the Auditor General pursuant to an address supported by 2/3rd of the majority of the State House of Assembly. Similarly, in ORISAKWE v. GOVERNOR IMO STATE[6] the plaintiff who was a recognized chief was removed

---

[4] (1985) 2 NWLR part 10 p. 806
[5] (1982) 3 NCLR 21
[6] (1982) 3 NCLR p.743

by the Governor of Imo State under the relevant chieftaincy and deposition law. Under the statute the Governor could only do this upon the advice of the Commissioner for Chieftaincy Affairs who must himself have set up a commission of inquiry to investigate the allegation of his conduct against the chief. No allegations were made against the plaintiff, no inquiry was set up and apparently no advice was given by the relevant Commissioner to the Governor, it was held that the Governor had acted in breach of the law.

In SHUGABA DARMAN v. MINISTER OF INTERNAL AFFAIRS[7] the plaintiff had been deported on grounds that he was not a citizen of Nigeria, it was argued on behalf of the Minister that since only the plaintiff's mother was a Kanuri, he was not a Nigerian citizen. The court held that the constitution did not distinguish between classes of citizenship by birth on all persons having a parent who is a Nigerian. The court therefore held that the deportation of the plaintiff was null and void.

This second exposition of the Rule of Law has been criticized on the ground that it does not recognize certain immunities or exemptions attaching to certain functionaries of the government, such as the President, Governors, Judges and Diplomats. These privileges cannot be arbitrary taken as they are necessary for the proper execution of their duties.

c. The third exposition of the Rule of Law according to Dicey is that rights guaranteed in the constitution of foreign countries is not derived from the constitution but rather arise inherently in the individuals. Dicey in this third proposition seeks to equate Rule of Law with divine law. This basic

---

[7] (1982) 3 NCLR P.915

proposition constitute the starting point of general analysis of the Rule of Law by other legal philosophers and writers. The International Commission of Jurists at several conferences has focused on the concept of Rule of Law. In 1955 the Commissioner at Athens conference emphasized the need for government to respect individual rights and provide effective means for their enforcement. The Commission at New Delhi in 1959 maintained this focus on individual right but particularized the right to extend to social, economic, cultural and educational conditions that would facilitate the realization of these rights.

Ultimately, the Rule of law has crystallized into the fundamental rights provisions which have been entrenched in the written constitutions of most countries in the world.

1. CONSTITUTIONAL SUPREMACY

A cursory look at succeeding Nigerian Constitutions depicts that the notion of Supremacy of Parliament is alien to our shores. In none of these constitutions is the absolute sovereignty of the local parliament recognized. Rather, the supremacy of the constitution has been a regular feature of our constitutions since the attainment of Independence. See Section 1(1) and 1(3) of the 1999 Constitution. The aforementioned provisions clearly emphasized that the constitution is supreme and by implication it is superior to the Legislature.

The Constitution of the Federal Republic of Nigeria 1999 clearly recognize the people as its creator thus ultimate authority resides in the people therefore it is the authority of the people over all organs of government created under the constitution that these legal basis for the supremacy of the constitution. One question that may be asked is why is the constitution made supreme over all other laws? The rationale for this is best illustrated by the decision of the United States Supreme Court in MARBURY v. MADISON.* The relevant part of the decision is reproduced below for ease of reference:

> It is a proposition too plain to be contested that the constitution controls legislative acts repugnant to it, or that the legislature may alter the constitution by an ordinary act. Between these alternatives there is no middle ground. The constitution is either a superior, paramount law, unchallenged by ordinary legislative act or like other acts it is alterable when the legislature shall please to alter them. If the former part of the alternative be true, then the written constitutions are absurd attempt on the part of the people to limit a power which in its own nature is illimitable.

By making the constitution supreme, what is intended to be accomplished or achieved? The answer can be found in the nature of the constitution. The constitution contains the terms and conditions under which all the different groups in the country agree to be governed. It describes the various institutions of the government, the relationship between different organs and the right of the citizens. It also distributes power and functions among the different levels of government. It imposes limits on the exercise of power by the different organs and levels of government.

If the constitution is not supreme it will have the same legal status as ordinary legislation and as such it could be

---

* 1 CR 137 (1803)

amended or even repealed by an ordinary law of the central legislature. This would have the effect that the legislature could at any time alter the system of government established by the constitution. Without the supremacy of the constitution there would be no assurance that the basic constitutional structure would be preserved. To provide this assurance, it is the major purpose why constitutions are made supreme. Commendably, the Nigerian court in a plethora of judicial decisions reiterated the supremacy of the constitution. See DOHERTY v. BALEWA,[9] WILLIAMS v. MAJEKODUNMI,[10] ADESANYA v. PRESIDENT[11] and MOMOH v. SENATE[12]

2. SEPARATION OF POWERS

Traditionally power is divided between the Legislature, the Executive and the Judiciary. The rationale for the doctrine of separation of powers can be found in the writings of Montesquieu, a French Jurist who observed thus:

> Every man invested with powers is liable to abuse it and carry his authority as far as to go... to prevent this, it is necessary from the nature of things that one power should be a check on another.

Another foremost philosopher John Locke based his view on the observation of the conditions prevalent in the seventeenth century England. The practice in vogue then was the divine rights of kings. In an attempt to curtail the absolute powers of the monarch, Locke developed the concept of social

[9] (*Supra*)
[10] (*Supra*)
[11] (1981) 1 NCLR p.236
[12] (1981) 1 NCLR p.21

contract in other to justify the notion of limited government. Locke observed that it may indeed be too great a temptation for human frailty to grasp power when the same person who has the power of making laws, also has the power to execute them. He then concluded that such a person may exempt himself from the obedience of the law. Although the diffusion of authority among different centre of decision making is the essence of the concept of separation of powers and consequently the antithesis of absolutism, it must be realized in the lights of the British and American models that some overlapping functions of the various agencies is sometimes inevitable. This should however be seen as a qualification and not a negation of the principle. In the Nigerian case of OJUKWU v. LAGOS STATE GOVERNMENT[13] the Court of Appeal held that the action of the government in evicting the plaintiff from his lodge amounted to an affront on the judicial function of the court as established under the Section 6 of the constitution and thereby a contravention of the principle of separation of powers. In SULE BALOGUN v. ATTORNEY GENERAL LAGOS[14] the High Court of Lagos State declared unconstitutional the legislation of the Lagos State House of Assembly which provided that the Governor of the State should create Local Government Councils contrary to the constitutional provisions that the creation of local governments must be preceded by judicial inquiry. The court therefore held that the provision of the law amounted to the usurpation of the judicial function of the court and a violation of the concept of the principle of separation of powers. See the

---

[13] (*Supra*)
[14] (1981) 2 NCLR p.589

following cases ADESANYA v. THE PRESIDENT,[15] GOVERNOR OF KADUNA STATE v. HOUSE OF ASSEMBLY,[16] OKWU v. WAYAS[17] and ATT. GENERAL OYO STATE v. ADEYEMI[18]

One can conclude by saying that historically, the doctrine of separation of powers stemmed from the observations of John Locke of the conditions prevalent in the 17th century England. But the doctrine as it is understood today is due to the work of a French Jurist Montesquieu who was primarily concerned with the preservation of that which in his view can only be found when there is no abuse of power by those in government.

3. FEDERALISM

Federalism is a constitutional device by which the powers of a state within a country are shared among two or more levels of government. The foremost exponent of the principle of federalism is Professor K. C. Wheare. He deduced the principle from his analysis of the essential features of the American Constitution which he considers an example of a perfect federalism. According to K. C. Wheare, federal principle means:

> The manner of dividing power so that the general and regional governments are within its sphere, coordinate and independent.

---

[15] (*Supra*)
[16] (1981) 2 NCLR p.144
[17] (1981) 2 NCLR p.522
[18] (1982) 3 NCLR p.846

Federalism is a complicated and delicate system of government. It is therefore important that in each country, the separating and uniting forces should be coordinated. This is because the essence of federalism is to have a common united government for certain purposes. It should not be the desire to create conflict and tension but rather to work in harmony for the achievement of a common good.

For federalism to work successfully, certain prerequisites must exist, there must be a written constitution which should be the supreme law of the country. A federation is formed as a result of an agreement between the federating unit and therefore it is essential that the terms of the agreement are reduced to writing so that there can be no doubt or ambiguity as to the terms of the agreement. The object of federalism is not to promote conflict and tension but to work in a harmonizing and cooperating way. It follows from this that there should be a body that will decide whether the action of a particular government is or is not constitutional such a power cannot be given to either of the parties to federalism, this is because any decision in the event of conflict or difference of opinion between the two levels of government may be acceptable when such decision is handed down by a body which is independent of the two levels of the government. This is why most federal constitutions have conceded this power of adjudication to the courts.

Where the power to pronounce on the constitutionality of legislation is entrusted to the courts, then the question of control over the appointment of judges assumes significance. In most federal constitutions the judges are appointed by the federal government with some sort of control given to the states. In Nigeria the power of adjudicating in respect of conflict are conferred on the courts but in the matter of appointments the states are given power to appoint high court judges once the central government appoints the judges of the Court of Appeal and Supreme Court.

REFERENCES FOR FURTHER READING

Ojo, A. (1987) *Constitutional Law and Military Rule in Nigeria.* Evans Brothers

Wade, H.W.R. (1982) *Administrative Law,* Oxford University Press, 5th edition

Shyllon, F & Obasanjo, O., *The demise of the Rule of Law in Nigeria under the Military: Two points of view*

Dicey, A. V. (1959,) *Introduction to the study of the law of the Constitution* 10th edition.

Chapter 3

HISTORICAL DEVELOPMENT OF NIGERIAN CONSTITUTIONAL LAW

BACKGROUND TO CONSTITUTIONALISM

Nigeria began in 1849 with the appointment of Mr. John Beecroft as the British consul to the Bights of Benin and Biafra. The consul whose assignment was the protection of British traders in the coastal areas had his headquarters in Fernando Po.

In 1851, the British bombarded Lagos in order to suppress the flourishing slave trade centre built by the Portuguese. This was followed in 1852 by a treaty signed between a British representative, Henry William Bruce and King Akintoye of Lagos for abolition of slave trade, encouragement of legitimate commerce and protection of Christian missionaries.

But the sudden death of King Akintoye in 1953 led to the enthronement of his son Docemo as the successor. King Docemo was unable to stop the flourishing slave trade along the coast of Lagos. Consequently, the British Government decided to occupy in order to effect a complete suppression of slave trade, give great aid and support to the development of lawful commerce and check the aggressive spirit of the King of the neighbouring Dahomey who was dealing in slave trade. Thus, King Docemo was persuaded to cede Lagos to the British crown in 1861. This gave the British their first effective foothold in Nigeria. From Lagos the British sent a number of expeditions to the hinterlands. This led to a declaration of British protectorate over the whole of Yoruba land except Abeokuta. The new protectorate was merged with the colony of Lagos.

Between 1862 and 1866, Lagos had its legislative and executive councils. From 1866-1874, the settlement of Lagos was merged with other British possession in West Africa to form the West African settlements with the headquarters in Sierra-Leone.

From 1874 to 1886, Lagos and the Gold Coast were separated from the other settlements with the Gold Coast Colony under a Governor based in Accra. By 1886, however, Lagos was re-established as a separate colony with its own Governor, executive and legislative councils. The latter council had power to provide for giving effect to His Majesty's jurisdiction in the protectorate of Lagos by ordinances, rules and regulations. In the same year the British entrusted the administration of the oil rivers protectorate hitherto in the charge of British Council to the Royal Niger Company. The company extended its sphere of influence to cover most of the present day Mid-West and Eastern States. Meanwhile Captain Fredrick Lugard had through a series of treaties with natural rulers and military expeditions brought most of Northern Nigeria under British rule.

In 1900, there was the declaration of Protectorate of Southern and Northern Nigeria and the merger of the Oil

Rivers Protectorate with the Protectorate of Southern Nigeria.

By 1906 the Colony and Protectorate of Lagos was merged with the Protectorate of Southern Nigeria.

In 1914, the two protectorates of Southern and Northern Nigeria were amalgamated with Sir Fredrick Lugard as the first Governor-General. After amalgamation, powers of the legislative council were confined to Lagos. The Governor-General was empowered to make laws for the protectorates. Instead of a legislative council for the whole country, an advisory and deliberative council - the Nigerian Council, was established to allow for consultation of local opinion before legislation. The council consisted of 17 officials and 13 unofficial all of whom were nominated by the Governor-General. The unofficial members were nominated by the Governor-General. The unofficial members nominated are as follows:

1. Four to represent commercial, shipping, mining and banking interest;
2. The Lagos Chambers of Commerce, the Calabar Chambers of Commerce and the Chambers and Mines appointed one member each;
3. The remaining six represented native populations and they were the Alafin of Oyo, the Emirs of Kano and Sokoto, Hon. C. A. Sapara-Williams, Chief Numa of Warri and Benin Rivers, Chief Henshaw of Calabar.

The inadequacy of African representations together with the ineffectiveness of the Nigerian Council gave rise to the introduction of Clifford's Constitution.

CLIFFORD'S CONSTITUTION

The constitution established a legislative council for Nigeria but its powers were confined to making laws for Southern Nigeria. The Governor-General retained the power to legislate for Northern Nigeria by means of proclamation.

Under the 1922 Constitution, every member of the legislative council could introduce or initiate legislation, but finance bills could only be introduced by the Governor-General. The real importance of the Legislative Council lay in the fact that it could debate any bill. However, because of the permanent majority of official members it was impossible to defeat the government on any measure. The composition of the Legislative Council consisted of the Governor-General as President and 46 members made up as follows:

1. 26 Officials members;
2. 15 Nominated members;
3. 4 Elected members from Lagos and 1 from Calabar.

This marked the introduction for the first time ever, of elective principles into Nigerian legislature. The main qualifications for standing election under this constitution were as follows:

i. the person should be an adult male British subject;
ii. he should possess property qualification of £100 (pounds) per annum;
iii. he must be resident in Lagos or Calabar for one year preceding election.

RICHARD'S CONSTITUTION OF 1946

The next constitutional milestone was the Richard's Constitution. The only significant modification introduced under the Richard's constitution was the introduction of regionalism into Nigeria namely: North, East and West with provision for Regional Houses of Assembly and House of Chiefs.

The Richard's Constitution established for the first time a legislature for the whole country. The composition of the Legislative Council consisted of the Governor-General as president; 15 official members; 28 unofficial members. The legislature for the first time contained unofficial majority. The Legislative Council had the power to legislate for the whole country. The regional assemblies established under the constitution had no real legislative powers of any kind. They were mere advisory bodies. The conditions for qualification for standing election under the earlier 1922 Constitution were preserved.

However, the financial qualification was reduced from £100 (pounds) to £50 (pounds) per annum.

The Executive council under the Richard's constitution was different from the earlier one. For the first time, 4 unofficial Nigerian members were nominated.

MACPHERSON CONSTITUTION 1951

The Macpherson Constitution of 1951 was not in fact the effort of Sir John Macpherson. The only justification for referring to it as the Macpherson Constitution appears to lie in the fact that the constitution became operational during his regime.

The constitution was designed essentially to avoid the criticism of the Richard's Constitution namely: that there was no adequate consultation with the people.

The striking features of the Macpherson Constitution included a central legislature called the House of

Representatives, a central executive called the Council of Ministers, which was presided over by the Governor.

Legislative and executive councils were also established for each of the then *three* regions. The central legislature comprising 136 elected members (34 each from the East and West and 68 from the North) enjoyed a wide legislative power while the regional assemblies legislated only in respect of designated subjects.

It was also a feature of this constitution that no bill of a regional assembly would receive the assent of the Governor until it had been sent to the central executive council for approval.

Election into the regional Houses of Assemblies were indirect. They were conducted through electoral colleges right from the village level until provincial representatives were elected to the regional Houses. The regional Houses themselves act as electoral colleges for elective regional members of the House of Representatives. The main qualification required of electors and candidates was that they were tax payers and satisfied the residential qualification of 12 months residency preceding the election.

1954 FEDERAL CONSTITUTION

This constitution is the product of two conferences held in London in 1953 and in Lagos in 1954 by Nigerian political leaders. The constitution made significant changes in the constitutional equilibrium of the country. Under this constitution, Nigeria became a federation of *three* Regions. The Constitution contained *two* legislative lists — the Exclusive and Concurrent lists. With regard to matters in the concurrent list both federal and regional governments could legislate within their specific spheres, and where there was any conflict, the law enacted by the federal government prevailed. All matters not on the lists were residual matters within the legislative competence of the regions.

The House of Representatives consisted of 184 elected members: (92 from the North, 42 each from the East and West, 2 from Lagos and 6 from Southern Cameroon).

The system of indirect election introduced by the 1951 constitution was discarded for direct election to the regional houses. The central council of ministers consisted of 10 ministers with 3 ex-officio members — Attorney General, Financial Secretary and Chief Secretary. The ministers were for the first time given departmental responsibilities.

The Civil Service and the judiciary were regionalized and Lagos was separated from the Western Region and constituted the Federal Territory. The Federal Supreme Court was established for Nigeria. High Courts were established for each of the regions and Lagos.

Following the constitutional conferences held in London in 1957, 1958 and 1960, leading to the Independence of Nigeria, a constitution contained in British-Nigeria (constitution) Order-in-Council 1960 was enacted.

1960 AND 1963 FEDERAL CONSTITUTIONS

It is generally agreed that both the independence constitution of 1960 and the Republican Constitution of 1963 introduced into Nigeria what is usually referred to as the "Westminster Model" constitutions.

The broad outlines of this model are patterned on the British constitution. It is that system of government in which there is a division of executive power between a ceremonial

Head of State and a Prime Minister: In such a system power in fact rests with the Prime Minister and his cabinet of ministers who are usually collectively and individually responsible to a freely elected legislature of which they must also be members.

The other broad outline of this sort of constitution is the inclusion of fundamental human rights and the limitations of parliamentary sovereignty. The constitution is recognized as the fundamental supreme law. The supremacy of the constitution also leads to another broad feature namely: the judicial determination of the validity of legislation.

Another feature of the 1960 and 1963 constitutions is the extent to which by use of certain institutional devices, some areas have been insulated from political influence such areas include the electoral commission, an independent Judicial Service Commission of which the Chief Justice was Chairman, and an independent Police Service Commission.

Other features are the inclusion in the constitutions of the convention governing particularly the exercise of judicial power, which in Britain remains unwritten, the inclusion of a detailed and justifiable bill of rights.

Perhaps, the more important feature of the Westminster constitution is the institutionalization of an opposition complete with a recognized leader as well as recognized representation in all committees of parliament, and the right to consultation by the Prime Minister before certain appointments are made.

Many African countries of the Commonwealth including Nigeria, found the Westminster model constitution grossly inadequate. The effect of the checks and balances inherent in the system was at best to make the art of governance extremely slow and lacking in direction and drive and at worst to make it impossible. Perennial personality conflicts and other institutional bottlenecks did not render the system to a developing society anxious to deal with the problems of poverty, hunger and illiteracy.

The separation of a Head of Government and Head of State was contrary to African traditional forms of government. The late Constitutional Affairs Minister in Kenya, Tom Mboya put it this way:

> We are an African State within the African family. This fact must be reflected both in the forms and in the reality of our government...This arrangement (by which you have a constitutional president and someone else as Head of government) is just not understood by our people, it is foreign to them. The historical process by which in other lands, Heads of State, whether Kings or Presidents, have become figureheads are not part of our African tradition. So in this respect we politely reject the West Minster Model.

Against this backdrop, it must be emphasized that the notion of a Chief who reigned but did not rule was unimaginable in traditional society. The Chief occupied a place of unique privilege and authority in the tribe. He was absolute monarch in both fact and name.

As for the institutionalized opposition of the Westminster model, this was certainly alien to traditional African society. An organized opposition was looked upon as a rebellious group and treated as such. Consensus was the hallmark of decision making in the traditional society. Such consensus over all issues facing the society was arrived at after long deliberations. It was during such deliberations that an individual could contribute constructive ideas.

The constitutional drafting committee prior to the enactment of the 1979 Constitution, set down the rationale for rejecting the Westminster model embodied in the 1960 independence and 1963 Republic Constitutions thus:

> The separation of the Head of State from the Head of Government involves a division between real authority and formal authority. This division is meaningless in the light of African political experience and history...

1979 FEDERAL CONSTITUTION

Many African countries of the Commonwealth including Nigeria, took the path of presidentialism because of the inadequacies of the Westminster model constitutions. In Nigeria, the 1999 Constitution came into effect on 1st October 1979 after almost 14 years of military rule in the country.

The constitution is unique in the sense that it is a departure from both 1960 and 1963 constitutions. Indeed it may be described as autochthonous since it is indigenous having been made by Nigerians themselves.

The broad outlines of that constitution are its introduction of:

1. a presidential democracy based on multi-party system;
2. the single executive both at the national and state levels;
3. the separation of powers between the three great departments of state - the legislature, the executive and the judiciary;

4. the inclusion of a comprehensive and judicable bill of rights;
5. the inclusion of the innovative and optimistic clauses on fundamental objectives and directive principles of state policy;
6. the inclusion of two main legislative lists — exclusive and concurrent legislative lists with residual matters left to the state;
7. considerable power is granted to the judiciary under the constitution;
8. the constitution also recognised political parties (sections 201 -209)

Section 122-161 deals with the vast executive powers given to the President, whilst section 162-172 contain executive powers of Governors in the states. The structure of the central legislature under the 1979 Constitution is bi-cameral, i.e., the National Assembly consists of *two* houses of equal status namely:

i) Senate with 96 members; and
ii) House of Representatives with 450 members.

EVOLUTION OF 1999 CONSTITUTION

Since the military struck again in December, 1983 and assumed the mantle of governance, resulting in the termination of the Second Republic, several attempts have been made by the military to fashion out or evolve an enduring constitution for Nigeria. Thus, the move towards evolving the present Constitution, i.e. 1999 is traceable to the inauguration in 1986 of the Political Bureau by the then military leader, General Ibrahim B. Babangida, whose main objective was to fashion out a proper, enduring and everlasting political arrangement for Nigeria. Prior to the Political Bureau, Nigeria had experimented in the first and Second Republics, the two most popular systems of government, i.e. Parliamentary and Presidential respectively. The Political Bureau headed by Retired Justice Cookey, submitted its report in 1987. The Bureau recommended the Presidential arrangement and the retention of Federalism, all as practiced under the constitution. In furtherance to these recommendations, a Constitution Review Committee was set up in 1987 to review the 1979 Constitution. Also, in that regard, a Constituent Assembly made up of elected and nominated representatives of Nigerians was established in 1988 to ensure the emergence of a new lasting constitution, acceptable to all Nigerians. The result of all these efforts was the emergence of the 1989 Constitution. This constitution did not however come into existence as the political arrangement, which was to constitute the basis of its effectiveness collapsed with the failure of the transition programme — that was to usher in the new political system. This was in June, 1993. The then military administration have attained the peak of the transition with the election into the office of the President conducted, annulled the elections. The chaos and restlessness that followed, ended what would have been regarded to as the Third Republic. Thus, the 1989 Constitution saw the light of the day. One major area of difference between the 1979 and 1989 Constitution was the entrenchment into the later of the two party system as opposed to the multi-party arrangement of the 1979 Constitution.

The annulment of the 1993 presidential elections resulted in a political arrangement that is similar to the 15th

January, 1966 handover of the governance of this country to the Armed Forces by the then civilian government by the Acting President Late Sir Nwafor Orizu. In the case of the 1993 handover, however, it was by the military to the civilian, although in a manner not also within the contemplation of the 1979 Constitution. It is submitted however that, although the change was not within the provisions of the 1979 Constitution, the existing grundnorm then was the Constitution (suspension and modification) Decree No. 17 of 1985 [1] and if the change was brought about by a Decree of the Federal Military Government, then to that extent the Interim National Government (ING) which was the arrangement brought into existence as a result of the election crisis of 1993, is valid.

The I.N.G. appeared unable to resolve the problems that arose from the annulment of the June 12, 1993 presidential elections, and while their mandate was amongst others, to ensure the conduct of another free and fair elections and return the country to a democratic rule through a process of election, the Army struck again and seized power from the I.N.G. which held forth for only *three* months.

The Army took over on 17 November, 1993. The new military regime of General Sani Abacha was unable to contain the various calls and insistence by Nigerians for a democratic rule. It wasted no time in initiating another process of ensuring a return to democracy. The Federal Military Government in 1994 inaugurated the Constitutional

---

[1] The Judiciary of recent has asserted the Supremacy of the Decree over the Constitution as exemplified in numerous cases like A.G. ANAMBRA STATE AND 13 OTHERS v. A.G. FEDERATION AND 16 OTHERS (1990 2 NWLR (Pt 130) 87).

Conference, which resulted in the 1995 Draft Constitution. The draft Constitution was essentially and substantially also based on the 1979 Constitution in terms of the form and structure of government. It recommended a multi-party system and the creation of more states and local governments. In 1996, more states and local government were created to bring the number to the present 36 states while new local governments were created to bring the number to the present 768 local government areas in Nigeria.[2]

The 1995 draft Constitution was eventually enacted as the 1999 Constitution with the demise of General Sani Abacha and the emergence of General Abdulsalami Abubakar in May, 1998. The twelve months old regime of General Abdulsalami Abubakar initiated a transition programme. The transition came to an end in May 29, 1999 with the handing over of power to a democratically elected civilian government of Chief Olusegun Obasanjo and which also marked the effective date of the 1999 Constitution.

ALTERATIONS TO THE 1999 CONSTITUTION

There have been some constitutional alterations since the promulgation of the 1999 Constitution. Although the alterations do not relate specifically to the issues discussed in the essays however, they deserve mentioning. So far, the alterations to the constitution are three (3). For the ease of reference the alterations are adumbrated below:

1. The Constitution of the Federal Republic of Nigeria (First Alteration) Act 2010. The Act alters the Constitution of

[2] See the Provision of Section 3(1) and (6) of the 1999 Constitution

the Federal Republic 1999 to among other things provide for financial independence to the Independent National Electoral Commission.

2. The Constitution of the Federal Republic of Nigeria (Second Alteration) Act 2010. This Act further alters the constitution to among other things provide for new time-lines for the conduct of national elections by the Independent National Electoral Commission.
3. The Constitution of the Federal Republic of Nigeria (Third Alteration) Act 2010. This Act alters the provision of the Constitution of the Federal Republic of Nigeria for the establishment of the National Industrial Court under the constitution.

REFERENCES FOR FURTHER READING

Odumosu, O. T. (1963), *The Nigerian Constitution: History and Development,* Sweet & Maxwell London.

Aihe, D. O. (1985), *Selected Essays on Nigerian Constitutional Law*

Coleman, J. S. (1958), *Nigeria Background to Nationalism,* University of California Press.

Ezera, K. (1960), *Constitutional Developments in Nigeria* Cambridge University Press.

Oluyede, P. A. O. (1992), *Constitutional Law in Nigeria* Evans Brothers.

Chapter 4

FUNDAMENTAL OBJECTIVES AND CONCEPT OF CITIZENSHIP UNDER NIGERIAN CONSTITUTION

FUNDAMENTAL OBJECTIVES AND DIRECTIVE PRINCIPLES OF STATE POLICY

At one time, it was thought that the state was mainly concerned with the maintenance of law and order and the protection of civil and political liberties. Such a restrictive role of the state is no longer a valid concept. We are, today, living in an era of a welfare state, which seeks to promote the wellbeing of the people. In order to establish such a welfare state, directive principles provide one of the most novel and striking feature in modern constitutional government.

Historically, the Republic of Spain took the lead in introducing the concept in its constitution. The idea subsequently found its way into the Irish Constitution of 1937. In 1948, India borrowed the idea into its Constitution. In Commonwealth Africa, the directive principles of state policy first appeared in the 1960 Republican Constitution of Ghana.

In Nigeria, the 1979 Constitution can be regarded as the very first attempt of introducing directive principles into our constitution. Both the 1960 and 1963 Constitutions were content with entrenched provisions of civil and political liberties. They contained no indication of any set goals for the country.

The entire Chapter II of the 1999 Constitution consisting of 10 sections, deal with the fundamental objectives and directive principles of state policy. These cover a wide range of spate activities for the realization of noble ideals given in the preamble to the constitution. Strangely enough, the constitution neither defines nor distinguishes the fundamental objectives from the directive principles. What is certain is that they contain certain goals to be pursued by the government and its agencies. They also impose certain obligations on the state to take positive action in certain directives in order to promote the welfare of the people. What then then is the rationale behind the objectives and principles?

Hedge and Mukharjea whilst writing on the utility of the principles in the Indian Constitution, made the following pertinent remarks, which incidentally, highlighted the aim of our own provisions:

> The fundamental rights and the directive principles constitute the conscience of our Constitution. The purpose of the fundamental rights is to create an egalitarian society, to free all citizens from coercion or restriction by society and to make liberty available for all. The purpose of the directive principles is to fix certain social and economic goals for immediate attainment by bringing about a non-violent social revolution. Through such social revolution the constitution seeks to change the structure of the society. It aims at making the masses free in the positive sense.

> Without faithfully implementing the Directive Principles, it is not possible to achieve the welfare state contemplated by the constitution.

It is thus, clear from the foregoing, that the principles and objectives stipulate the objectives of the state and the principles, which must guide its policies. They also stipulate the minimum standards required to achieve a just, free and contented society.

At this juncture, a review of some of these objectives will be very illuminating.

Political

Sections 14 and 15 of the Constitution conjunctively touch on the political goals of the Nigerian State when it deduced that the Federal Republic of Nigeria should be a state based upon the principles of democracy and social justice. Sovereignty is also vested in the people who are endowed with the right to participate in Government. The need for the reflection of federal character in state policy is also emphasized.

Consequently, in the composition of the federal government or that of a state, it must be ensured that there is no predominance of persons from a few states or from a few ethnic or other sectional groups. Thus, national unity and integration is elevated over and above sectional and other parochial interests.

Economic

Section 16 enjoins government to ensure the even economic development of the country in order to secure maximum welfare for the good of the people. In order to achieve this goal, the government is given the control of Economic resources of the country.

Social

The social objectives spelt out in section 17 include the provision of social security, the provision of fair living conditions for workers and the protection of the weak.

Education

Section 18 enjoins government to ensure equal opportunity in educational matter and also promote literacy among the people. To achieve this goal, government is enjoined to provide free and compulsory universal primary education immediately and free education at all levels as soon as practicable.

Foreign Policy

Section 19 states that the government should promote international cooperation, combat racial discrimination and promote African Unity.

Culture

In section 21 the government is enjoined to protect and enhance Nigerian culture. The phrase "Nigerian Culture" is not easy to decipher given the very diverse and varying cultural background of the Nigerian people.

NON-JUSTIFIABILITY OF OBJECTIVES AND DIRECTIVES

Evidently, these are ideals and objectives in the best tradition of a welfarist state. However, the most serious source of objection to the whole concept is the fact that these principles and objectives are non-justiciable. If these objectives are indeed essential to establishing the egalitarian state, why is no machinery put in place for enforcing compliances by the organs and agencies of the state?

It should be recalled that section 13 of the Constitution provides:

> It shall be the duty and responsibility of all authorities, and persons exercising legislative, executive and judicial powers to conform to, observe and apply the provisions of that chapter of the constitution!!

In so far as the legislative and Executive organs are concerned, the fundamental objectives and directive principles can be easily given effect to.

As for the judiciary, it is highly regrettable that section 6 (6)(C) of the Constitution completely insulates the directives and objectives from judicial review, how then can the judiciary give effect to them?

The Court of Appeal in OKOGIE v. ATTORNEY-GENERAL[1] (LAGOS) suggested that the courts through its interpretative jurisdiction, can give effect to the directives by adopting the view that will be in conformity with the objectives. The thinking of the court is that the entire laws can be brought in line with the objectives through such approach. The limitation of this suggestion becomes very glaring where the courts in a given case, must give a literal interpretation to a statute, which is contrary to the fundamental objectives.

In our view, this dilemma would have been avoided if a clause akin to section 6(2) of the Republican Constitution of

---

[1] (1981) 2 NCLR 218

Ghana had been inserted in the 1999 Constitution. The Section provides thus:

> The government shall report to parliament at least once a year all the steps it has taken to ensure the realization of the policy objectives contained in this chapter, and in particular, the realization of a healthy-economy, the right to work, the right to good health care and the right to education.

CITIZENSHIP

The legal position of Nigerian citizenship established under the 1960 Constitution remained largely the same under the Republican Constitution that entered into force on 1st October, 1963. Even when the military intervened in 1966 by suspending and modifying the existing Constitution, the provisions relevant to the Nigerian citizenship remained intact. However, by the time the first presidential constitution was produce in 1979, the provisions relating to the acquisition of the Nigerian citizenship had undergone appreciable modifications. The relevant provisions in the 1999 Constitution were slightly amended by the 1989 Constitution and the 1995 Draft Constitution. Since the 1999 Constitution introduced most of the major innovations, the relevant provisions thereunder will be restated; while the subsequent modifications under the succeeding constitutions will be reflected. Under the 1999 Constitution, there are three main ways by which the citizenship of Nigeria can be acquired. These are:

a. By birth - section 25;
b. By registration – 26; and

c. By naturalization - section 27,

In principle these ways did not seem to differ from those under the 1960 and 1963 Constitutions.

Citizenship by Birth

Under, the 1999 Constitution, the following persons are citizens of. Nigeria by birth, namely:

a. Every person born in Nigeria before the date of independence, (i.e., 1st October, 1960) either of whose parents or any of whose grandparents belongs or belonged to a community indigenous to Nigeria: Provided that a person shall not become a citizen of Nigeria by virtue of this section if neither of his parents or any of his grandparents was born in Nigeria.

b. Every person born in Nigeria after the date of independence either of whose parents or any of whose grandparents is a citizen of Nigeria; and

c. Every person born outside Nigeria either of whose parents is a citizen of Nigeria.

Citizenship by registration

(1) Subject to the provisions of section 28 of the 1999 Constitution, a person to whom the provisions of this section apply may be registered as a citizen of Nigeria, if the President is satisfied that:

a) He is a person of good character;

b) He has shown a clear intention of his desire to be domiciled in Nigeria; and

c) He has taken the oath of allegiance prescribed in the sixth schedule to the 1999 Constitution.

(2) The provisions of this section shall apply to:

(a) Any woman who is or has been married to citizen of Nigeria; or

(b) Every person of full age and capacity born outside Nigeria any of whose grandparents is a citizen of Nigeria.

Citizenship by naturalization

(1) Subject to the provisions of section 28; of the 1999 Constitution, any person who is qualified in accordance with the provisions of this section may apply to the President for the grant of a certificate of naturalization.

(2) No person shall be qualified to apply for the grant of a certificate of naturalization, unless he satisfies the President that-

(a) He is a person of full age and capacity;
(b) He is a person of good character;
(c) He has shown a clear intention of his desire to be domiciled in Nigeria;
(d) He is, in the opinion of the Governor of the state where he is or he proposes to be resident, acceptable to the local community in which he is to live permanently, and has been assimilated into the way of life of Nigerians in that part of the federation;
(e) He is a person who has made or is capable of making useful contribution to the advancement, progress and wellbeing of Nigeria;
(f) He has taken the oath of allegiance prescribed in the sixth schedule to the 1999 Constitution; and
(g) He has, immediately preceding the date of his application, either –

i. Resided in Nigeria for continuous period of 15 years; or
ii. Resided in Nigeria continuously for a period of 20 years, immediately preceding that period of 12 months, he has resided in Nigeria for periods amounting in the aggregate to not less than 15 years.

Avoidance of Dual Citizenship Section 28 of the 1999 Constitution

(1) Subject to the other provisions of this section, a person shall forfeit forthwith his Nigerian citizenship if he acquires or retains the citizenship or nationality of a country other than Nigeria;

(2) Any registration of a person as a citizen of Nigeria or the grant of a certificate of naturalization to a person who is a citizen of a country other than Nigeria at the time of such registration or grant shall be conditional upon effective renunciation of the citizenship or nationality of that other country within a period of not more than 12 months from the date of such registration or grant.

(3) A citizen of Nigeria by birth shall not forfeit his Nigerian citizenship if, within 12 months of the coming into force of the provisions of this chapter or of his attaining the age of 21 years (whichever is the later) he renounces the citizenship or nationality of any other country which he may possess.

Deprivation of Citizenship Section 30 of the 1999 Constitution

1. The President may deprive a person, other than a person who is a citizen by birth or by registration, of his citizenship, if he is satisfied that such a person has within a period of 7 years after becoming naturalized been sentenced to imprisonment for a term of not less than 3 years.

2. The President shall deprive a person, other than a person who is a citizen of Nigeria by birth, of his citizenship, if he is satisfied from the records of proceedings of a court of law or other tribunal, or after due inquiry in accordance with regulations made by him, that

(a) The person has shown himself by act or speech to be disloyal towards the Federal Republic of Nigeria; or

(b) The person has, during any war in which Nigeria was engaged, unlawfully traded with the enemy or been engaged in or associated with any business that was in the opinion of the President carried on in such a manner as to assist the enemy of Nigeria in that war, or unlawfully communicated with such enemy to the detriment of or with intent to cause damage to the interest of Nigeria.

Persons deemed to be Nigerian citizens Section 31 of the 1999 Constitution

A parent or grandparent of a person shall be deemed to be a citizen of Nigeria if at the time of the birth of that person such parent or grandparent would have possessed that status by birth if he has been alive on the date of independence, i.e., 1st October, 1960.

Power to make regulations Section 32 of the 1999 Constitution

1. The President may make regulations not inconsistent with these provisions prescribing all matters which are required or permitted to be prescribed or which are necessary or convenient to be prescribed for carrying out or giving effect to the provisions of this chapter, and for granting special immigrant status with full residential rights to non-Nigerian spouses of citizens of Nigeria who do not wish to acquire Nigerian citizenship.

2. Any regulations made by the President pursuant to the provisions of this section shall be laid before the National Assembly.

REFERENCES FOR FURTHER READING

Akande, J. O. (1982), *The Constitution of the Federal Republic of Nigeria 1979,* Sweet & Maxwell, London.

Oluyode, P. A. O. (1992), *Constitutional Law in Nigeria,* Evans Brothers.

Chand, H. (1980), *Nigerian Constitutional Law,* Santosh Publishing House, New Delhi.

Chapter 5

REFLECTIONS ON THE NATURE OF FUNDAMENTAL RIGHTS

A legal right is that which the law protects and which can be enforced in courts of law. It is the right, which is protected and enforced by the ordinary law of the land. But there exist other rights which stand above the ordinary laws of the land and which are antecedent to the political society itself. These rights are, indeed, primary conditions to any civilized existence in societies governed under a written constitution, these rights are not protected, but are also guaranteed by that constitution. These rights are termed fundamental rights because not only are they primary conditions to civilized existence, but while the ordinary laws of the land which can be freely altered or changed by the legislature, they cannot easily be altered by parliament.

HUMAN RIGHTS DISTINGUISHED FROM FUNDAMENTAL RIGHTS

Some writers employ interchangeably the terms 'human rights' and fundamental rights'. For the sake of clarity, it is appropriate to note the distinction between both. In this connection it is apposite to refer to the clear distinction drawn by late Justice ldigbe in a paper, which he presented at the All

Nigerian Judges Conference in 1982. The learned Justice drew the distinction this way:

> It must be pointed out at this stage that those rights which are antecedent to the political society itself do not exist only in societies or states with written constitutions. By their very nature, they exist also in states or political societies without any written constitutions. However, unless their existence or continued existence is guaranteed under the state's constitution they cannot with reference to that particular state or political society, be described as fundamental rights. It is therefore my respective view that a description of these rights as fundamental rights ought to be confined to states or political societies governed by written constitutions.

It follows from the foregoing, that while all rights enjoyed and asserted by human persons may be described generally as human rights; not all human rights can be termed fundamental rights.

Human rights are as old as the society itself for they derive their existence from the need of the human person, as a rational being, to live, develop and realize the essential humanity of the person. Indeed, human rights are basic conditions to rational and civilised living, and it behoves the state to ensure that the law recognizes many of these rights.

However, history teaches us that human rights do not just happen, and very often, the people have had to struggle and at times, fight for their rights. Throughout history, people in different countries as well as international bodies have asserted and declared solemnly what they believe to be just and suitable content of human rights.

Examples of national declarations of human rights and freedom are:

1. The Bill of Rights of England (1689) which established the force of the general law, the supremacy of parliament over the Crown, and provided for freedom against imprisonment or detention by the command of the sovereign without good cause;
2. The American Declaration of Independence (1776) which proclaimed equality of man and his unalienable rights to life, liberty and the pursuit of happiness;
3. The Declaration of the Rights of Man and of the Citizen adopted by the French National Assembly in (1789) which proclaimed liberty, equality and fraternity of the people.

On the international plane, concern for protection of the human rights was triggered off by the horrendous events of the Second World War, which culminated in the systematic elimination of the Jews. This forced humanity to think seriously about human rights. Invariably, the aftermath of the Second World War gave impetus to international human rights movements.

The Universal Declaration of Human Rights, which constitutes the most comprehensive and central document on the course of human rights, was adopted on the 16th of December 1948 by the General Assembly of the United Nations.

Regrettably the Universal Declaration of Human Rights was not accompanied by an effective system of control such as judicial machinery guaranteeing the effective promotion of these rights. Consequently, the idea of regional organizations gained rapid prominence where states were unable to find general solutions to the problems confronting them in the field of human rights.

The emergent regional organizations were to create a climate conducive to the initiation and development of joint ventures in the field of human rights. Indeed, it would appear that regionalism is the key to the problem of effective protection of human rights today.

The fine achievements of the European Convention of Human Rights, the American Convention of Human Rights, as well as, the African Charter on Human and Peoples Rights are significant milestones in promoting human rights. These efforts cumulatively influenced the constitutional entrenchment of Bill of Rights in emergent states.

CONTENTS OF FUNDAMENTAL RIGHTS

The fundamental rights guaranteed in the Independence Constitution of 1960, the Republican Constitution of 1963, and the current Constitution of 1999, are eleven in number. They are entrenched in chapter four of the 1999 Constitution of the Federal Republic of Nigeria and their content is spelt out in sections 33-46 of the Constitution.

The guaranteed rights to be examined in this lecture are: The Right to life, Right to dignity of human person, Right to fair hearing and Right to privacy.

(i) Right to Life

Almost all Constitutions in the civilised world now guarantee the right to life. Section 33 of the 1999 Constitution of the Federal Republic of Nigeria guarantees the right to life to every person. A cursory look at the section depicts that the word "life" is nowhere defined. The word has not been judicially interpreted in any Nigerian case that one is aware of. We are therefore necessarily guided by the decisional gloss placed on the word by the American Supreme Court, which is reproduced here for ease of reference:

> By the term here used, something more is meant than mere animal existence. The inhibition against its deprivation extends to all those limbs and facilities by which life is enjoyed. The provision equally prohibits the mutilation of the body or amputation of an arm or leg or the pulling out of an eye or destruction of any other organ of the body through which the soul communicates with the outer world.

This view of the word "life" by the American Supreme Court is a classic statement, which is accepted in all subsequent judicial decisions.

Having positively conferred the right to life on every person, Section 33 of the 1999 Constitution goes on to provide: "No person shall be deprived of life except in the following cases."

First, under Section 33(1) life can be intentionally deprived in the execution of the sentence of a court in respect of a criminal offence for which a person has been adjudged guilty in Nigeria. This limits on Section 33 seriously undermines the right to life in that it leaves it open to the legislature to enact laws providing for the deprivation of life in any case it likes. The courts merely award sentence only when such is prescribed by a law enacted by the legislature.

Second, in Section 33(2), a person may be justifiably deprived of his life if he dies as a result of the use of such force and in such circumstances as is permitted by law. The use of force must be reasonably necessary in the circumstances spelt out in paragraphs a — c of section 33 (2) namely:

(a) For the defence of a person from unlawful violence or for the defence of property;

(b) In order to effect a lawful arrest or prevent an escape from lawful custody; and

(c) For the purpose of suppression of riot, mutiny or insurrection.

It should be emphasized that the deprivation of life in the circumstances noted above must be reasonably necessary for achieving the objectives contained in paragraphs a-c. By importing the objective test of reasonableness, the courts are unwittingly conferred with wide powers to determine in every given case whether deprivation was reasonably necessary.

Third, if the abridgements to the right to life contained in the limbs to section 33 are not enough, Section 41(2) provides specifically that during an emergency - such as in the extreme case of an act of war, the deprivation of life can be justified. See BELLO v. ATTORNEY GENERAL OYO STATE.[1]

(ii) Right to Dignity of the Human Person

This right is guaranteed in section 34 of the 1999 Constitution. After spelling out the right in such general terms in Section 34(1), the section goes on to specify in paragraphs a-c, certain practices the prohibition of which is necessary to accord respect to human dignity. The inhuman practices mentioned specifically are: (a) torture or inhuman or degrading treatment; (b) slavery and servitude; (c) forced or compulsory labour.

---

[1] (1986) 5 NNLR 828

In order to appreciate the purport of this provision, it will require that interpretation of some expressions used therein be attempted. The word "dignity" appears very elastic and its content can be determined by reference to the prevailing state of civilization, morals and ethics of the Nigerian Society at any given point in time. What is certain, however, is that the dignity referred to is not that of a highly sensitive person or that of a person with hardened sensibility. It is the dignity of a reasonable man.

The phrase "torture, inhuman or degrading treatment" refers to the well-known practice of torturing human beings or doing things offensive to their body sensibilities and so on

The word "slavery" refers to the institution of slavery as known in history. The additional word "servitude" is used in the constitution to guard against the possible practice of other species of slavery that might evolve in human relations at different times.

As for the phrase "forced or compulsory labour", it relates to those practices under which persons are subjected through physical coercion to do a particular work under the pains of penalty amount to forced or compulsory labour. These include:

(a) any labour required in consequence of the sentence or order of a court;

(b) any labour required of members of the Armed Forces or Police or a substituted service for conscientious objectors;

(c) any labour required during national calamity for the wellbeing of the community;

(d) any labour required that forms part of normal communal or other civil obligation for the welfare of the community or such compulsory service in the armed forces or national service which forms part of the education and training of Nigerian citizens.

In the Nigerian case of ALHAJA ABIBATU MAGAJI v. BOARD OF CUSTOM & EXCISE,[2] the court deprecated the crude practice adopted by the respondent in raiding markets as offensive to human dignity.

(iii) Right to Personal Liberty

This is undoubtedly the most controversial of all the rights guaranteed in Chapter Four of the 1999 Constitution. Its controversial status derives from the frequency with which its contents are modified and suspended by successive military juntas.

Section 35(1) broadly confers on every person the right to personal liberty. The constitution, however, does not define what constitutes personal liberty. On a cursory look it would appear from the phraseology of the section that it confers solely to freedom from any form of physical or bodily restraint. The premise for such construction can be gleaned from the literal interpretation of the world "liberty" which is qualified by the word "personal".

In ADEWOLE v. JAKANDE,[3] the court gave a liberal interpretation of the section when it held inter-alia that a circular of the Lagos State Government abolishing private primary schools, infringed upon the liberty of parents to direct the upbringing and education of their children.

There are six grounds listed in section 35(1) upon which personal liberty can be abridged. These are spelt out in

[2] (1982) NCLR 552

[3] (1981) 1 NCLR 262

paragraphs a - f thereof and are adumbrated below for ease of reference:

a. Personal liberty can be abridged in the execution of a sentence or order of a court where a person has been found guilty of an offence under the criminal law. This exception is meant to facilitate the administration of criminal justice;
b. Personal liberty can be abridged also where a person fails to comply with the order of the court or fails to discharge an obligation imposed by law;
c. Personal liberty can also be abridged for the purpose of bringing a person before a court upon reasonable suspicion of his having committed an offence or as may be necessary for preventing a person from committing an offence;
d. In EGAJI UJAH v. ATTORNEY-GENERAL BENUE STATE[4] the court held the view that where the charge before a court does not rest upon reasonable suspicion, a citizen's personal liberty cannot be allowed to be interfered with by the prosecution, especially if there is no reasonable ground to justify that a criminal offence has been committed;
e. Persons suffering from infectious or contagious diseases or persons of unsound mind, or drug or alcoholic addicts, or even persons who are vagrants may be deprived of their personal liberty for the purpose of their care or treatment or for the protection of the community;
f. Personal liberty may also be deprived for the purpose of preventing unlawful entry into Nigeria, or effecting expulsion, extradition or other lawful removal from Nigeria.

---

[4] (1982) 3 NCLR 330

Aside from the foregoing exceptions, Section 45(2) provides also that personal liberty can be derogated from during any period of emergency.

Section 35(2) provides, albeit limitedly, the right from self-incrimination when it states that a person arrested or detained can remain silent until after consultation with a legal practitioner or any other person of his own choice.

(iv) Right to Fair Hearing

Section 36 of the 1999 Constitution deals with the right to fair hearing. The Constitution does not define by the phrase "fair hearing": Notwithstanding this lacuna, it is submitted that the phrase substantially incorporates the common law doctrine of natural justice and its components.

Section 36 draws a distinction between the concept of fair hearing in civil proceedings and criminal proceedings. Section 36(1)-(3) provide for fair hearing in civil proceedings. Section 36 (1) provides:

> In the determination of his civil rights and obligations including any question or determination by or against a government authority, a person shall be entitled to fair hearing within a reasonable time by a court or other tribunals established by law and constituted in such a manner as to secure its independence and impartiality.

The expression "civil rights and obligations" has not been defined in the Constitution. We are therefore guided by the decisional gloss placed upon an analogous phrase by the Federal Supreme Court in MERCHANT BANK v. FEDERAL

MINISTER OF FINANCE.[5] In that case, the Federal Supreme Court took the view that the right to licence to do banking business under the Banking Ordinance does not come within the meaning of civil right. What can be gleaned from this decision is that Nigerian courts construe the expression rather narrowly as legal rights, thus excluding privileges.

See also the following decisions: OBARIOGE v. GOVERNOR OF ONDO STATE;[6] ORISAKWE v. GOVERNOR OF IMO STATE.[7]

On what constitutes a "reasonable time" within the purview of Section 36(1), it was held in FALADE v. ATTORNEY GENERAL LAGOS STATE[8] that no hard and fast definition of the expression can be proffered. "Reasonable", time, therefore must depend upon the peculiar facts of each case.

Section 36(4) generally confers the right to fair hearing on an accused in criminal proceedings.

Section 36(5)-(12) broadly spell out the minimum requirements that must be met in the course of criminal proceedings. See generally FAWEHINMI v. LEGAL PRACTITIONERS DISCIPLINARY COMMITTEES[9] and ANYAH v. ATTORNEY-GENERAL BORNO STATE[10]

(v) Right to Privacy

Section 37 of the 1999 Constitution provides that the privacy of the citizens, their homes, correspondence, telephone

---

[5] (1961) 1 All NLR 598
[6] (1982) 3 NCLR 349
[7] (1980) 3 NCLR 743
[8] (1981) 2 NCLR 771
[9] (1982) 3 NCLR 719 47
[10] (1984) 5 NCLR 401

conversation and telegraphic communication, is hereby guaranteed and protected.

It would appear that the rationale for providing for the right to privacy stems from the need to protect the purely private affairs of the individual so as to facilitate the development of the individual to the best possible extent. It is of course recognized that there are certain basic things which are private in nature and which no person would like to reveal to others.

In a legal commentary titled "The right to privacy", Warren and Brandels made me a strong case for the constitutional guarantee of the right to privacy thus:

> Instantaneous photographs and newspaper enterprise have invaded the scared precincts of private and domestic life and numerous mechanical devices threaten, to make good the prediction that what is whispered in the closet shall be proclaimed from the house tops...The press is overstepping in every direction the obvious bounds of propriety and of decency.

Although, there is yet no Nigerian decision on the subject it is obvious that if the right to privacy is widely interpreted, it would impinge on the freedom of expression, especially in relation to the press.

It should be pointed out that the right to privacy may be curbed by section 45(1) by a law which is reasonably justifiable in the interest of defence, public safety, public order, public morality or public health, or for protecting the rights and freedoms of other persons.

(vi) Freedom of Thought, Conscience and Religion

Section 38 of the 1999 Constitution guarantees the right of everyone to choose his own religion or ideology and to teach same to others, while at the same time not being forced to learn about any religion other than your own. Under normal circumstances, the government does not interfere with this right except where there is a breach of the peace by a preacher. Section 38 also prohibits secret societies. See JENEBU ONYE v. ALEYI ANEGBUDU.[11]

(vii) Right to Freedom of Expression

This is one of the indices for assessing a democratic society. The rationale for entrenching the right in the Constitution stems from the need to allow everyone in the society to hold any opinion or idea and to communicate the idea to others.

Section 39(1) of the 1999 Constitution confers the freedom to hold opinions and to receive and impact ideas and information on every person.

Section 39(2) makes it clear that this freedom includes the right to own, establish and operate any medium for the dissemination of such information, ideas and opinions. However, in respect of radio and television stations, no person other than the Federal or State Governments, or such person as authorised by the President, can own and establish or operate any wireless and television station for any purpose whatsoever.

Section 39(3) states that the freedom is subject to the limitation as may be imposed by law provided that such restriction is reasonably justifiable in a democratic society:

---

[11] (1983) NCLR 492

(a) For the purpose of preventing disclosure of information received in confidence, or to maintain the authority and independence of the courts or for regulation of wireless broadcasting, television or the exhibition of cinematographic films; or

(b) For preventing public officers and members of the armed forces from disclosing information.

Aside from the restrictions contained in Section 39, Section 45 of the Constitution permits further restrictions in the interest of defence, public order, security, morality and health.

The scopes of the freedom of expression and the permissible restrictions that may be imposed therein have been examined in a plethora of decisions. In TONY MOMOH v. SENATE,[12] the then Editor of the *Daily Times* Newspaper was summoned by the Senate to disclose sources of information contained in the article in which Senators were accused of lobbying for contracts from the executive arm of government. The Editor refused to disclose the source of his information on the ground that Section 39(2) extended the protection contained in Section 39(1) to the content of any medium for the dissemination of information, ideas and opinion which includes publications in newspapers.

The decision in that case reiterated the fact that freedom of the press is no more or less than the freedom of expression of the individual and that the constitution does not recognize any privileged position for the "press". The word "press" only connotes a medium for imparting information, ideas and

[12] (1982) 1 NCLR 105.

opinion of editors and publishers. It is therefore amply covered by the word "medium" used in Section 39.

In OYEGBAMI v. ATTORNEY-GENERAL OF FEDERATION,[13] the *Daily Sketch* published a story captioned "Armed Robbers kill 2 persons". The Editor was summoned by the Police and asked to disclose the source of the information. The Editor challenged the constitutionality of the Police action under Section 39 of the Constitution. The court held that, the press was one of the pillars of freedom in any nation; that the press report matters of general interest and cannot be compelled to disclose their source of information. The court further held that if editors and reporters are unable rely on the constitutional shield of confidentiality, the public will be denied the free flow of information. See also ADIKWU v. FEDERAL HOUSE OF REPRESENTATIVES.[14]

In ATTORNEY GENERAL IMO STATE v. UKAEGBU[15] the defendant, without prior approval of the government attempted to establish a private educational institution called "Imo Technical University". He commenced the erection of buildings and called for application for admission. The government filed a suit seeking an order of injunction to restrain the defendant from establishing the institution without prior approval of the government. The court held that under section 39 of the Constitution, every citizen has the right to own, establish and operate any medium for the dissemination of information, idea and opinion including any

---

[13] (1982) 3 NCLR 895
[14] (1982) 3 NCLR 394
[15] (1981) 2 NCLR 568

school or institution for that purpose. See also OKOGIE v. ATTORNEY GENERAL LAGOS STATE.[16]

It should be noted, however, that the freedom of expression conferred on persons should not be construed as permitting the criticism of government in vitriolic terms such as to incite hatred or disaffection against the government. See generally: D.P.P. v. CHIKE OBI[17] and R. v. AMALGAMATED PRESS LTD.[18]

(viii) Right to Peaceful Assembly and Association

This right is conferred on every person by Section 40 of the Constitution. The right is essential in a democratic society with a multi-party system of constitution. Such right will not be available, for instance, in a one-party state. The section also allows employees or members of a profession to organize themselves into labour or trade union to protect and further their interest.

Note, however, that the right is only in respect of political parties recognised by the Electoral Commission and also that this right cannot be invoked by an elected member in a legislative house to change his party before the next election. Section 40 is subject to any law made in the interest of defence, public safety, and public order. See generally CHERANCI v. CHERANCI.[19] In this case, the question before the court was whether some section of the Children and Young Person's Law of the Northern State of Nigeria were void on the grounds of being unconstitutional. The said section prohibited children

---

[16] (1981) NCLR 218
[17] (1961) All NLR 186
[18] (1961) All NLR 199
[19] (1960) NLR 24

under fifteen years from participating in any political activity and also makes it an offence to admit such under aged in any party as members. The court refused to hold the said section as an unjustifiable infringement of a fundamental right. The right conferred in Section 40 may be limited where the Police refuse to permit, to hold public meetings or processions which may lead to commission of some criminal wrongs such as breach of peace, unlawful assembly, rioting and public nuisance.

(ix) Right to Freedom of Movement

Section 41(1) confers a general right on every citizen of Nigeria or to reside in any part thereof. It also prohibits the expulsion of any citizen from Nigeria. No citizen may also be refused entry or exist from the country.

Section 41(2) states that a person's freedom of movement can be restricted in accordance with a law that is reasonably justifiable in a democratic society so as to: (a) prevent such person from leaving Nigeria where he has committed or is reasonably suspected of committing crime; and (b) to extradite a person from Nigeria to any country to face trial or to serve a sentence of a court for criminal offence where a treaty of reciprocity exists.

In SHUGABA DARMA v. FEDERAL MINISTER OF INTERNAL AFFAIRS,[19] it was held that a Nigerian citizen cannot be deported from Nigeria and that the Immigration Act of 1963, was inconsistent with Section 41 of the 1979 Constitution and is therefore void.

Note that any order curtailing citizens' freedom of movement must be proved to be reasonably justifiable; if it is not, the court would declare it unconstitutional. See ROTIMI

WILLIAMS v. MAJEKODUNMI[20] and ADEGBENRO v. ATTORNEY GENERAL.[21] Note also, that freedom of movement can also be restricted in other circumstances. For example, in the case of an infant he can be put in custody for his protection, education or care. A person can be detained to prevent the spread of contagious diseases or for mental illness; alcoholics and drug addicts may also be incarcerated.

For non-citizens or illegal immigrants, they can be detained so as to depot or extradite them.

(x) Right to Freedom from Discrimination

Section 42(1) of the 1999 Constitution provides that no citizen of Nigeria should be discriminated against by reason only of belonging to a particular community, ethnic group, place of origin, sex, religion or political opinion.

Section 42(2) prohibits the subjection of any Nigerian citizen to any disability or, deprivation merely by reason of the circumstances of his birth.

Section 42(3) provides an exception. That is, in respect of a law imposing restriction with respect to the appointment of any person to any office under the state or as a member of the Armed Forces of the Federation or a member of the Nigeria Police Force or to an office in the service of a body corporate established directly by any laws in force in Nigeria.

(xi) Right to Property

Section 43 of the Constitution gives what may be described as a right to property to citizens in that it prohibits any compulsory acquisition of citizens property except in the

[20] (1962)
[21] (1962) 1 All NLR 431

manner and for the purpose prescribed by a law. The section also gives the individual; right for compensation on the property acquired in accordance with a law. See CHERANCI v. CHERANCl.[22]

Note that Section 43(2)(f) contains the doctrine of "Police Power" in that, government can take over property that constitutes a menace to public welfare without giving compensation.

LIMITATIONS OF ENJOYMENT OF FUNDAMENTAL RIGHTS

Section 45(1) of the 1999 Constitution states that all rights guaranteed under Sections 37-41 can be derogated and restricted in the interest of defence, public safety, public order, public morality, or public health. Those rights may also be derogated or restricted for the purpose of protecting the rights and freedoms of other persons. The reasonableness of any such restriction can be challenged in court.

Section 45(2) states that in the case of those rights guaranteed in sections 33-36 of the Constitution, they can be restricted only in a period of emergency. A period of emergency is defined in Section 45(3) as any period during which there is in force a proclamation of a state of emergency declared by the President in the exercise of the power conferred on him pursuant to Section 305 of the Constitution.

As it is, almost all the rights mentioned in chapter four of the constitution can be derogated from in accordance with Section 45 by a "democratic society".

---

[22] *Supra*

This expression is quite elastic and may be invariably abused. In practice (at least during civilian dispensations) what one can discern from judicial authorities is that the courts have consistently reiterated that the determination of what is "reasonably justifiable" is the exclusive preserve of the courts. See generally; CHERANCI v. CHERANCI,[23] DPP v. CHIKE OBI[24] (1961) and WILLIAMS v. MAJEKODUNMI[25]

In the final analysis, the cumulative effect of all the exceptions or derogation is to take away with the left hand what was given with the right. The question one is therefore left with is, is there any real guarantee of the right? Put differently, is it necessary to entrench these rights in the Constitution? Opinions differ on the answer to this question. Some support qualified guarantee because it allows government to discharge its duties or functions. An extreme view is that in developing countries like Nigeria, we do not need Bills of rights and that what is needed is a guarantee to work, food, education, health and shelter.

All in all, even though the entrenched rights may give some false sense of security, it is desirable to still have the rights in the Constitution.

ENFORCEMENT OF AND REMEDIES FOR BREACH OF FUNDAMENTAL RIGHTS

Section 46 of the 1999 Constitution creates a special jurisdiction for the High Court of a state with regard to the enforcement of fundamental rights. Section 46(1) provides that any person who alleges that any of the provisions of

[23] *Supra*

[24] (1961) 1 All NLR 186

[25] (1962) 1 All NLR 413

chapter four has been, is being or likely to be contravened in any state may apply to a High Court in that state for redress.

This is a very wide provision in that it covers not only cases of actual violations of fundamental rights but also cases of anticipated breach of right. In OKOGIE v. ATTORNEY GENERAL LAGOS STATE,[26] the Attorney-General contended inter-alia that the right of the plaintiff had not been infringed and consequently, it was premature for him to have instituted the action in court. The court overruled this contention when it held that Section 46(1) permits a plaintiff to commence proceedings if he fears that his right is likely to get trampled upon.

Section 46(2) of the Constitution gives the High Court original jurisdiction to hear and determine any such application and the court may make such order, issue such writ or give such direction as it may consider appropriate. Undoubtedly, this provision confers latitude of discretion on the courts to determine the appropriateness of the order to be made.

In Section 46(3) of the Constitution the Chief Justice of the Federation is empowered to make rules with regard to practice and procedure for the enforcement of fundamental rights.

Section 46(4) of the Constitution empowers the National Assembly to confer additional powers on the courts that may be necessary for effective enforcement of the fundamental rights. The sub-section refers to "orders, writs and directives" to be given by the High Court in order to give redress to an aggrieved person. These orders, writs and directives are,

---

[26] (1981) 1 NCLR 218

however, not specifically spelt out. It is submitted that the constitutional expression refers to the prerogative writs and orders as understood in English law, examples of which include Habeas Corpus, Mandamus, Certiorari and Prohibition. This contention finds support in the liberal attitude of the courts in their approach to matters relating to the enforcement of the guaranteed rights.

This liberal approach was successfully articulated by Fatai-Williams C.J.N. in SOKEFUN v. AKINYEMI & ORS[27] as follows:

> I take the view that because it is so fundamental to the life and liberty and wellbeing of the individual, it should be possible for any person who complains about an alleged infringement of any of his fundamental rights as entrenched in our constitution to canvas the issue of such infringement at any stage of any court proceedings, whether in the trial court or on appeal.

At this juncture, it is desirable to discuss briefly these prerogative writs and orders because of their profound importance and relevance in matters related to fundamental rights.

(i) *Habeas Corpus*

This is the swiftest constitutional remedy where the liberty of a citizen is in jeopardy. It is in the nature of an order made by a court directing the person or authority having custody of a person, to produce that person in court or show under what legal authority that person is being detained.

---

[27] (1980) 5 SC 1

When the detaining authority files a return in response to the writ showing the legal authority for the detention, the court will proceed to determine whether the detention is justifiable or not. Where the detention is justifiable, the immediate order for the release of the detainees is made by the court. See generally: LIVERSEIGE v. ANDERSON[28] and AGBAJE v. COMMISSIONER OF POLICE.[29]

(ii) Mandamus

This is an order issued by the court to a person or authority having a public duty, to perform that duty in accordance with and in the manner prescribed by law. It will, therefore, only issue to compel the performance of a public duty that is, a duty imposed by law. The performance of such duty must, however, be mandatory and it will not issue if the performance of the duty is discretionary. See the following: R v. COMMISSIONER FOR LAGOS AFFAIRS EXPARTE CHERUBIM & SERAPHIM;[30] R. v. WESTERN URHOBO RATING AUTHORITY EX PARTE ODJE.[31]

Note that only a person who has a right or interest in the performance of the public duty can apply to court for an order of mandamus - see BANJO v. ABEOKUTA U.D.C.

(iii) Certiorari

This is unarguably one of the most effective remedies in constitutional law. It is a writ issued by the High Court to a court of tribunal of subordinate jurisdiction, directing it to send the record of the proceedings before it for the

---

[28] (1942) AC 206
[29] (1969) NMLR
[30] (1960) 1 LLR 123
[31] (1961) 1 All NLR 716

determination of its legality. The writ can be used to quash or set aside the decision of an inferior court or tribunal where the proceedings before it are patently wrong in law, or, are in excess of jurisdiction.

The scope of the writ was examined by Lord Atkin in R. v. ELECTRICITY COMMISSIONER[32] thus:

> Whenever anybody or person having legal authority to determine questions affecting the rights of the subject, and having duty to act judicially acts in excess of 'its powers, it will be subject to the supervisory or controlling jurisdiction of the Kings Bench Division.

In certiorari, the superior court is not sitting on appeal but merely determines whether the subordinate tribunal has confined itself to the jurisdiction given to it, or whether it has committed an error of law, which is apparent on the face of the record, or whether it has violated any principle of natural justice. If the proceedings are quashed, the matter is referred back to the inferior tribunal for proper adjudication. See: BOARD OF EDUCATION v. RICE,[33] OKPAKU v. RESIDENT PLATEAU PROVIN CE[34] and ARZIKA v. GOVERNOR NORTHERN REGION.[35]

(iv) Prohibition

This writ is issued by a court to an inferior tribunal of subordinate jurisdiction to discontinue proceedings before it. The requirements of this writ are substantially the same as

[32] (1965) NMLR 295
[33] (1911) AC 179
[34] (1985) N. N. L. R. 5
[35] (1961) All NLR 379

those of Certiorari except in one respect - Certiorari is issued when the lower court has already concluded the case and made a finding, whereas, prohibition is issued before the conclusion of a case. The superior court intervenes swiftly to correct any illegality so that the subsequent proceedings in the lower court will be conducted in accordance with law. It should be noted that application for both Certiorari and Prohibition can only be made at the instance of a person who has a legal interest in proceedings before the lower court, or person whose right is adversely affected in any way by, the determination of the proceedings in the lower court.

REFERENCE FOR FURTHER READING

Chand, H. (1980), *Fundamental Rights,* Santosh Publishing House, New Delhi.

Akande, J. O. (1982), *The Constitution of the Federal Republic of Nigeria,* Sweet & Maxwell, London

Oluyede, P. A. O. (1992), *Constitutional Law in Nigeria,* Evans Brothers

Chapter 6

LEGISLATIVE POWERS UNDER THE NIGERIAN CONSTITUTION

The legislature is the supreme law-making organ of the state. The National Assembly under the 1999 Constitution is bi-cameral in nature in that it is composed of the Senate and the House of Representatives. The state legislature is unicameral in nature.

MEANING AND SCOPE OF LEGISLATIVE POWERS

Legislative power is the power to make laws. In a Federation, this law-making power is usually shared by levels of government, that is, the central and state legislature.

Section 4(1) of the 1999 Constitution vests the legislative powers of the federation on a bicameral legislature collectively referred to as the National Assembly. This assembly comprises two chambers, namely, the Senate and the House of Representatives.

Section 4(2) of the Constitution empowers the National Assembly to make laws for "the peace, order and good government of the federation or any part thereof." The expression "Peace, order and good government" has not been judicially interpreted in Nigeria. Consequently, one can only be guided by the construction placed on an identical expression contained in the Canadian Constitution by the

Judicial Committee of the Privy Council in the case of RUSSEL v. QUEEN.[1] In this case, the thrust of the argument was whether an Act of the Canadian Parliament which prohibited the sale of liquor except for some specified purposes was ultra vires the power of parliament. Under the Canadian constitution, civil rights and property holding are matters within the legislative competence of the provinces. In upholding the validity of the Act of Parliament in question the Privy Council stated, *inter alia*:

> What Parliament is dealing with in legislation of this kind is not a matter in relation to property and civil right but one in relation to public order and safety.

That is the primary matter dealt with and though accidentally in the free use of things in which we may have property is interfered with, that accidental interference does not alter the order of things.

From the foregoing passage, what is evident is that the expression "peace, order and good government" is quite fluid and confers a great deal of latitude upon the central legislature. This expression can thus be utilized to expand the powers of the central legislature to any extent.

An attempt is made in Section 4(3) and (4) to spell out the scope of the legislative competence of the National Assembly. The National Assembly is empowered to legislate exclusively on the matters listed in part one of the second schedule to the Constitution. In respect of the matters contained in Part Two of the Second Schedule to the Constitution, both the central and state legislatures may make

---

[1] (1882) L.R. 7 App. Case 827

laws concurrently on those items. Section 4(5) spells out that where there is any inconsistency between the laws of both legislatures on a concurrent matter that of the central legislature prevails.

Under section 4(6) the legislative powers at the state levels, are vested in the House of Assembly of the state. This Assembly is unicameral in nature with powers to legislate on matters contained in the concurrent legislative list as well as on residual matters.

A cursory look at the provisions of the 1999 Constitution shows that the scheme on the distribution of legislative powers between central and state legislatures can only be disturbed in three circumstances:

a. If the country is at war, the central legislature gets the competence to legislate on all subjects aside from those contained in the Exclusive list; for the purpose of prosecuting the war section 11(3);
b. The central legislature is competent to make laws on a state subject whenever it becomes impossible for any given State House of Assembly to convene or hold its sittings and transact business. See section 11(4);
c. The central legislature is also competent to make laws even in respect of a state subject if it becomes necessary to give effect to a treaty obligation entered into by the Federal Government with a foreign country. See section 12(3).

RESOLUTION OF LEGISLATIVE CONFLICTS UNDER A FEDERAL SCHEME

In a federation, it is quite a common feature for both the central and state legislatures to make laws on specified subjects within their respective competence and such laws may inadvertently clash or conflict. Conflicts in the manner described above are in-built in every federal arrangement. For the swift resolution thereof, the courts have devised a number of constitutional doctrines; these are:

i. The doctrine of "pith and substance";
ii. Implied powers of doctrine; and
iii. Repugnancy or occupied field doctrine. Each is now examined in turn.

i. Pith and substance doctrine

The utility of this doctrine becomes apparent whenever a given legislature makes law on a subject within its competence and which law encroaches upon some aspects of the subject within the competence of another legislature. This possibility is indeed real since most legislative items are couched in broad outline form with no indication given as to the specific details thereof. Consequently, in order to effectively legislate upon a subject on the list, it may require also that all incidental matters be covered by such legislation.

In so doing, such legislation may unwillingly encroach upon the sphere of influence within the competence of another legislature. When this kind of situation occurs, the question normally, arises as to whether such legislation be declared invalid in so far as it has encroached upon the subject within the competence of the other legislature. What is certain is that if the former attitude were to be adopted by the courts, then obviously a great deal of legislations will get invalidated and the legislature may be unable to function effectively.

The courts therefore devised the "pith and substance" doctrine to remedy such anomalies. Simply put, the doctrine means that when a law passed by a given legislature is in "pith and substance" in respect of a subject within its competence, then such a law shall be valid in its entirety notwithstanding that it has incidentally strayed or encroached upon a subject, which is within the legislative competence of another legislature.

The application of this doctrine is clearly exemplified in the case of AKWULE & ORS v. THE STATE (*supra*). In this case, the appellant who was a bank official was tried and convicted for the offence of breach of trust under section 315 of the Penal Code (which is a statute enacted by the then Northern Region legislature to regulate criminal matters). The appellant challenged the validity of section 315 of the Penal Code on the ground that the regional legislature had no power to make law in respect of banking which is an item on the Exclusive List of the 1963 Constitution. The court clearly rejected the argument and upheld the validity of section 315 of the Penal Code by applying the doctrine of pith and substance.

In coming to its decision, the court found as a fact that in substance, the offence of criminal breach of trust by bankers punishable under Section 315 of the Penal Code was indeed a law in respect of a criminal matter notwithstanding that it encroaches upon banking which is a federal subject. See also RUSSEL v. QUEEN.

(ii) Implied power doctrine

This doctrine connotes that where the Constitution expressly confers on the legislature the power to make law on a given subject matter, the scope of the power impliedly extends to all those matters that are necessary for the effectuation of the power conferred.

The doctrine was laid down by the American Supreme Court in McCULLOCH v. MARYLAND.[2] Under the American Constitution, Congress is empowered to legislate in respect of the following:

(a) currency and legal tender;

(b) collection of federal revenue; and

(c) payment of federal funds

In that case, Congress passed a law authorizing of the establishment of a federal bank. The validity of this law was challenged on the ground that the powers of Congress are only those specified in the Constitution and that powers not so specified belong to the states. It was contended that since banking is not one of the specified subjects, the Congress exceeded its legislative competence and encroached upon a state subject.

The American Supreme Court rejected this contention and decided that the federal law was valid on the ground that the powers expressly granted to the Congress extended to such other matters as are natural and necessary for giving effect to the express power. The establishment of a bank for the deposit of federally collected revenue and for making payment from federal funds was therefore considered essential to a meaningful exercise of the expressly granted powers.

Under the 1999 Nigerian Constitution, the implied powers doctrine seems to have been accepted in items 67 and 68 of the Exclusive Legislative List. The constitution specifically states that the power of the federal legislature extends to matters incidental and supplemental to the powers expressly stated in the list. To make it abundantly clear, the

---

[2] 4 WHEAT 316 (1819)

constitution defines incidental and supplemental power to include offences, courts, and the acquisition of land.

(iii) Repugnancy doctrine

This doctrine is variously referred to as the doctrine of occupied field or covering the field. It emanated from the decisions of Australian and American Courts. Under the 1999 Constitution both the federal and state legislatures are competent to make laws in respect of concurrent subjects. Section 4(5), however, provides that if the state law is inconsistent with the federal law, the state law shall be void.

When the federal legislature has not made law in respect of a given matter, the state law will operate fully. Conflict only arises when both the federal and state legislatures one after the other, make law in respect of the same subject matter. The phrase "to the extent of inconsistency" appearing in section 4(5) of the Constitution would suggest that the state law can be invalidated only when it cannot stand together with the federal law on the given subject.

Literally construed, it is possible for a state law to supplement and fill in the gaps in the federal law and that being the case, both laws can co-exist. Such a literal view was initially taken by the American Supreme Court. The court, however, later changed its view and decided that where the federal legislature has made a law on a concurrent subject with a clear intention from the provisions thereof that its law alone should cover the subject, then any state law even if it is not inconsistent with the federal law will be invalid.

Strictly speaking, the foretasted view which was elaborated upon by the Australian High Court is not in accordance with the letters of the 1999 Constitution of

Nigeria, which only invalidates state laws "to the extent of its inconsistency"

Inconsistency between federal and state laws may arise in three different ways:

1. when both laws are in actual conflict such as when one permits an act, which the other prohibits, naturally, in such a situation, both laws cannot stand together;
2. the phraseology of both laws may not be in real conflict yet, inconsistency could arise in their actual operation. Both laws cannot in such an event also stand together;
3. when the central legislature also enacts a law making its intention quite emphatic that its law alone should occupy the particular field exclusively. In such an event, if the state law enters that field it becomes inconsistent with the federal law in so far as it enters upon the field. This is so even if the terms of the state law are not in direct conflict with the federal enactment.

In CHIROMA GIRAMBE v. BORNU NATIVE AUTHORITY,[3] the Federal Supreme Court applied the doctrine of inconsistency in the first sense considered above, namely, actual conflict.

In that case, section 13 of the Federal Supreme Court Ordinance, empowered the Federal Supreme Court to order the unconditional retrial of a case by the High Court. Section 185 of the Criminal Procedure Code of the Northern Region, however, confers jurisdiction to try a case on the High Court only when the case is committed to it by the Magistrate Court. There was thus a clear conflict between the provisions of Section 185 of the CPC and Section 13 of the Ordinance. This

---

[3] (1961)

is because when the Supreme Court orders an unconditional retrial by the High Court under Section 185 of the CPC, the High Court would have to send the case to the Magistrate who had the power to even order a discharge. The exercise of such power by the Magistrate will be clearly inconsistent with the unconditional order of retrial made on the Supreme Court. On this basis, therefore, Section 185 of the CPC was declared to be unconstitutional in so far as it derogates from the power of the Supreme Court under Section 13 of the Ordinance.

This doctrine was directly considered by the Supreme Court in the case of ATTORNEY GENERAL OF OGUN STATE v. ATTORNEY GENERAL OF THE FEDERATION (1961)[4] otherwise known as the "public order case". In this case, the Federal Military Government had passed the Public Order Act of 1979. At the time, the Federal power to make laws in respect of matters not within the exclusive list, subject to order conditions:

a) that a state law on a concurrent subject could be made with the prior approval of the Federal Government;
b) that any state law which is inconsistent with the federal law will be void.

When the 1979 Constitution came into force, the Public Order Act was an existing law and therefore, it could be adapted by the President or Governors under section 4 of that constitution. The President consequently amended the Act under this adaptation power. Some of the amendments conflicted with the public order laws of the States.

The validity of the adaptation power of the President was challenged on the ground that the Public Order Act of 1979

---

[4] (1982)

was in respect of a concurrent subject. It was argued that being a state subject only the State Governors had power to amend by adaptation.

The Supreme Court rejected this contention by the states by applying the covering the field doctrine. It then ruled that under the 1979 Public Order Act, the Federal Legislature evinced a clear intention that in matters of public order, only the federal law should occupy the field. The court declared all state laws on "public order" unconstitutional.

It should be noted that word "void" used in Section 4(5) connotes "in operative" or "dormant", such that if the Federal Act is repealed the state law becomes operational forthwith.

REFERENCES

Odumosu, O. T. (1963), *The Nigerian Constitution: History and Development*, Sweet & Maxwell London.

Aihe, D. O. (1985), *Selected Essays on Nigerian Constitutional Law*

Coleman, J. S. (1958), *Nigeria: Background to Nationalism,* University of California Press.

Ezera, K. (1960), *Constitutional Developments in Nigeria,* Cambridge University Press.

Oluyede, P. A. O (1992), *Constitutional Law in Nigeria,* Evans Brothers (1982)

Chapter 7

SCOPE OF EXECUTIVE POWERS UNDER THE NIGERIAN CONSTITUTION

The phrase 'executive powers' defies any uniform definition. It may simply be described as the power to administer the constitution and the laws of the country. The President, under the 1999 Constitution, is the embodiment of executive powers. He epitomizes the executive authority of the Federation. Governors also enjoy similar status in the states.

MEANING AND SCOPE

Section 5(1)(a) of 1999 Constitution vests the executive powers of the Federation in the President. The powers may be exercised directly by the President or through the Vice-President and Ministers of the government of the Federation, or through officers in the public service of the Federation.

The scope of executive powers under the Constitution extends to the execution and maintenance of the Constitution; all law of the National Assembly and all matters within the legislative competence of the National Assembly.

Section 5(2)(a) of the 1999 Constitution similarly vests the executive power of a state in the Governor of that state who may exercise the power directly or through his Deputy and Commissioners as well as through officers in the public service of the state. The provision of that section stipulates that the executive powers of a state cannot be exercised in a manner that will impede or prejudice the exercise of the executive powers of the Federation or endanger the continuance of a federal government in Nigeria.

The nature of the executive power under the 1999 Constitution became the subject of litigation in numerous cases. The question that fell to be decided in the cases centred on whether the Executive powers of the Federation or of a State are vested solely in the President or Governor; or whether power is for all purposes, vested in some other authority or body. In LAWAL KAGOMA v. GOVERNOR KADUNA STATE,[1] the question was whether the Governor could appoint a commission of inquiry only in compliance with or subject to commission of inquiry law of the state empowers the executive council of the state to appoint a commission of inquiry to investigate the affairs of local governments.

In this case, the Governor, acting on his executive authority under the constitution, had appointed a commission of inquiry. Consequently, the constitutionality of his action was challenged. Majority of the Court of Appeal held that under the local government law, only the executive council had the power to appoint the commission and not the Governor who is obliged to appoint an executive council under section 174 of the 1999 Constitution.

It was felt that since no executive council had been set up in Kaduna State, the Governor had not power to institute the commission of inquiry. The President of the Court of Appeal

---

[1] (1982) 3 NCLR 1032

observed that the Governor under the 1979 Constitution is not intended to be a dictator.

The view of the Court of Appeal restricting the power of the Governor was not approved on appeal to the Supreme Court. The Supreme Court took the view that it is the Constitution that has vested the executive powers in the Governor, which he may exercise directly or through other officials. The court conceded that the legislature may regulate powers but noted that in so doing, the legislature cannot divest the Governors of their constitutional powers.

POWERS AND FUNCTIONS OF THE PRESIDENT AND GOVERNORS UNDER THE 1999 CONSTITUTION

Aside from the general vesting of Executive powers in Section 5 of the Constitution, the Constitution also confers certain specific powers on Governors. These include the underlisted immediately below.

(a) Appointment and Removal

In matters of appointment, the 1999 Constitution has conceded to the President and Governors very limited powers. Appointment to cabinet positions are subject to confirmations of the legislature under Sections 147(2) and 192(2) of the Constitution. Other civil, judicial and police officers are appointable by their respective service commissions who also have the power to remove the appointees. The President's removal powers can only extend to the members of his cabinet, his special advisers and ambassadors. Other executive bodies have fixed tenures and their removal also could be only subject to legislative approval. (See, for example, Section 155 of the 1999 Constitution). The executive is not part of the legislature under a Presidential constitution like the 1999 Constitution. The President and Governors are elected directly by the people for a fixed tenure of four years. They can only be removed from office through impeachment process as prescribed in sections 143 and 188 of the 1999 Constitution.

The Ministers and Commissioners cannot be members of the legislature. If any of them is a member of the legislature, he is deemed under Section 147(4) to have vacated the seat on such appointment as Minister or Commissioner.

Since the executive is separated from the legislature under the constitution, the former cannot partake in the proceedings of the latter. Notwithstanding, the President or Governors may send draft bills and messages to the legislature from time to time. The legislature is however, not bound to consider such executive sponsored measures. Bills passed by the National Assembly or State Houses of Assembly only become law upon being assented to by the President or Governor as the case may be. The President or Governor has 30 days within which to give such assent or to withhold it. Where the executive assent is withheld the legislature can pass such bill into law by two-thirds majority.

(b) Powers in relation to foreign affairs

In matters of foreign relations, the President occupies an enviable position and the courts have generally shown reluctance to interfere with Presidential relations. The President appoints ambassadors after Senatorial confirmation. He negotiates and concludes treaties with foreign nations. However, any treaty concluded by the President shall not have the force of law unless it is enacted into law by the National Assembly.

c) Defence Power

The war powers of the President seem to be considerably limited. The President is the Commander-in-Chief of the Armed Forces. In that capacity he can direct and command the Armed Forces. There are, however, certain constitutional limitations imposed on the exercise of this power by the President.

First, section 5(4) of the 1999 Constitution states that the President shall not declare a state of war except with the sanction or resolution of the two houses of the National Assembly at a joint sitting.

In the matter of appointment to defence service, the President is vested with power under Section 218(2) of the Constitution. This power may, however, be regulated by laws made by the National Assembly.

d) Emergency Powers

Section 305 of the 1999 Constitution deals with the emergency powers of the President. Section 305(3) empowers the President to issue a proclamation of a state of emergency only when the following situations exist:

i. when the Federation is at war;
ii. when the Federation is in imminent danger of invasion or involvement in a state of war;
iii. when there is actual breakdown of public order and public safety in the Federation or any part thereof to such an extent as to require extraordinary measures to restore peace and security;
iv. when there is a clear and present danger of an actual breakdown of public order and public safety in the

Federation or any part thereof requiring extraordinary measure to arrest same;

v. when there is exists other public danger clearly constituting a treat to the existence of the Federation; or

vi. when the President receives a request to do so. Under section 265(4) of the Constitution, a state Governor with the approval of two-thirds majority of the State House of Assembly could request the President to declare emergency in a State. If the Governor fails to make such a request within a reasonable time, the President may declare emergency in such a state if there is breakdown of public order or security.

The President is required to send the National Assembly a copy of the proclamation immediately after it is issued. The declaration of emergency, will expire after two days if the National Assembly is in session or ten days, if not in session — where the National Assembly does not approve the proclamation. Where it approves the proclamation, it will be valid for six months and may thereafter be renewed by a resolution of the National Assembly for another further six months.

e) Police Powers

The maintenance of law and order is an item under the concurrent legislative list in the 1999 Constitution. In spite of this, Section 214 of the Constitution provides for the establishment of a single Nigerian Police Force under the control of the central or Federal Government. The Section prohibits the setting up of any other Police Force. Consequently, the states cannot establish their own Police Force for the maintenance of peace and order.

Under section 215(1), the Inspector General of Police is appointed by the President under whom the entire Police Force is placed. The President or the Minister in charge of Police Affairs may give lawful directions necessary for the maintenance of public peace and security in any part of the country. Governors enjoy similar powers in the states. However, Police Commissioners in the states are also empowered under the provisions of Section 215(4) to seek directions from the President or Minister in which case they need not comply with the directives of Governors. This provision enables the Police Commissioners to disregard directives from Governors at will once they have the support of the Federal Government.

f) Power in Relation to Prerogative of Mercy

Section 175(1) of the 1999 Constitution vests in the President power to pardon, commute, or remit sentences imposed on convicts. Similar powers are enjoyed by State Governors in respect of sentences for offences under their state laws. See Section 212 of the 1999 Constitution. When pardon is granted, the person is totally absolved in the eyes of the law and his guilt is wiped off. A pardon can be absolute or conditional in nature.

Commutation of sentence connotes that a lesser punishment is substituted in place of the sentence imposed by the court. For example, a death sentence may be reduced to life imprisonment and life imprisonment reduced to a number of years. In the case of remission, the unexpired portion of the sentence is waived and the prisoner is set free. It is usually granted as a result of good conduct in prison.

It is significant that section 175(2) of the Constitution enjoins the President to exercise the powers in consultation with the Council of State.

ATTORNEY GENERAL'S POWERS

Section 174(1) confers certain power on the Federal Attorney General. Similar provisions exist in section 211(1) for the Attorney General of a state. The constitutional powers are exercised by the occupants of the office independently based on their personal judgment rather than under the direction of their Chief Executives.

Under section 174(1) the Attorney General is conferred with power to:

i. Constitute and undertake criminal proceedings;
ii. Take over and continue any such criminal proceedings that may have been instituted by any other authority or person; or
iii. Discontinue at any stage before judgment is delivered in any criminal proceedings.

In section 160(2), the exercise of the power is subject to the following:

1. That the power is exercised by the Attorney-General in person or through officers in his department; and
2. That the power is to be exercised to prevent the abuse of legal process in the public interest.

In BALA KEFFI v. STATE[2] the Solicitor General entered a *nolle prosequi* at the High Court and the charge was terminated. The father of the victim of the crime filed a suit at the High Court for an order of declaration that the Solicitor

[2] BALA KEFFI v. STATE

General, in the absence of any delegation of power by the Attorney General, was incompetent to exercise the power under Section 191(1) of the 1979 Constitution and as such the termination of the charge was unconstitutional.

It was contended on behalf of the State that the Solicitor General could exercise the power since there was no Attorney-General in office at the time. The Court rejected his contention and held that only the Attorney General could exercise the power in person or by specifically giving instruction to an officer in his department in that regard.

In STATE v. ADAKOLE,[3] the Court of Appeal examined the nature of the power of the Attorney-General under section 191 of the Constitution and took the following view:

a. That it was wrong to construe section 143(3) to mean that the Attorney General must expressly give his reasons either orally or in a document filed before the court in entering a *nolle prosequi*;
b. That in exercising the power under section 191 of the Constitution, the Attorney General may be seen as a judicial officer who should be guided by considerations of public interest, justice and avoidance of the abuse of the legal process.

REFERENCES FOR FURTHER READING

Chand, H. (1981), *Nigerian Constitution,* Santosh Publishing. House, New Delhi.

Nwabueze, B. O. (1982), *A Constitutional History of Nigeria,* Longman.

[3] (1981) 2 NCLR 410

Ojo, A. (1987) *Constitutional Law and Military Rule in Nigeria*, Evans Brothers.

Oluyede, P. A. O. (1992), *Constitutional Law in Nigeria,* Evans Brothers.

Dicey, A. V. (1959), *Introduction to the study of the Law of the Constitution,* 10th edition.

Chapter 8

JUDICIAL POWERS AND CONCEPT OF JUDICIAL INDEPENDENCE UNDER THE NIGERIAN CONSTITUTION

MEANING AND SCOPE OF JUDICIAL POWERS

The term 'judicial power', like other legal concepts, is difficult to define. It may be described as the power, which the state exerts in the administration of public justice in contradistinction from the power it possesses to make laws and the power to execute them.

Most federal constitutions specifically confer judicial powers on the courts. However, there is no uniform set up of the organization of courts in federations. For example, in the United States, there is a dual system of courts. The state courts are distinct from the federal courts. In Nigeria, however, although the judicial power of the federation is vested in the Federal Courts and that of the State, in State Courts, there is yet one single hierarchy of courts.

Under the 1999 Constitution, the Court of Appeal and the Supreme Court are Federal Courts in the sense that appointment of their judges is made by the Federal Government whereas the judges of State High Courts are appointed by the State Government.

In most federations, Nigeria inclusive, the Supreme Court is the apex Court. It is conferred with original as well as appellate jurisdictions. The original jurisdiction is confined to disputes between the federation and States, or between the states *inter se*. In all other respects, the jurisdiction of the apex court is appellate.

The permissible scope of judicial powers under the 1999 Constitution can be deciphered from the contents of section 6(6). The phrase "civil rights and obligations" is capable of being construed widely not only as legal rights but also privileges, freedoms, and liberties. This expression invariably makes the question of *locus standi*, a precondition for the invocation of judicial powers at the instance of any complainant.

It is instructive that the sub-section also contains the expression "matters between government or authority and any person in Nigeria." The conjunctive reading of this part of the sub-section together with the former (that is, "civil rights and obligations") would suggest that only a party who demonstrates direct interest in the civil rights and obligations will have a standing in law to invoke judicial power to come to his aid.

On this score, it is commendable that the Supreme Court of Nigeria in ATTORNEY GENERAL BENDEL STATE v. ATTORNEY GENERAL FEDERATION[1] gave a broad construction to interest whilst upholding the standing of Bendel State Government in challenging the validity of the Revenue Allocation Act passed by the National Assembly ostensibly for non-conformity with the constitutional procedure for enacting laws. The court noted, *inter alia*, that the plaintiff had an existing right to a particular percentage of

---

[1] ATT. GENERAL BENDEL v. ATT. GENERAL FED (1982) 3 NCLR 166

revenue allocation; that where such right is sought to be disturbed by a measure purported to be a law of the National Assembly, the aggrieved State can contend that such a measure is not law in accordance with the provisions of the 1979 Constitution. Such a State would in the circumstance have a standing. See generally: MAIKARFI v. EZEOKE[2] and JIDEONWO v. GOVERNOR BENDEL STATE[3]

JUDICIAL REVIEW

This doctrine is a constitutional contraption devised for the control of abuse of governmental powers. It was propounded by the American Supreme Court in MABURY v. MADISON.[4] The doctrine essentially confers on the courts power to pronounce on the constitutional validity or otherwise, of a law enacted by the legislature. The doctrine is conceived of as necessary adjunct to a written constitution. It has been subject to a welter of criticism.

One view is that it is a "veto power" granted to the courts. Evidently, this view is misconceived as what the court does is merely to reject any retrogressive legislation which is inconsistent with the constitution. The doctrine does not elevate the courts to the status of a super-entity.

Another view is that the doctrine negates separation of powers, being a circuitous exercise of legislative power by the courts. Again, this view is misconceived. Aside from pronouncing on the constitutionality of the legislative measure, the courts do not introduce substitutes. Despite the formidable assaults unleashed upon the doctrine, it is crystal

---

[2] (1980)
[3] (1981) 1 NCLR
[4] *Supra*

clear that it is an indispensable tool in modern constitutional government. The doctrine, however, can only flourish in a country where there is legalism, that is to say, where the courts are given what may be aptly described as freedom of justice.

Under the 1999 Constitution of Nigeria, judicial review is an implied power and not a substantive power as no specific section of the constitution provides for judicial review. A cursory look at the following constitutional provisions depicts pointedly that judicial review is an implied power under the 1999 Constitution:

i) Section 1(3) declares unmistakably that any law which is inconsistent with the provisions of the constitution shall be void to the extent of its inconsistency;
ii) Section 4(8) provides that the exercise of legislative power shall be amenable to the jurisdiction of the courts and judicial tribunals established by law;
iii) Section 6 projects the predominance of the judiciary under the constitution;
iv) Lastly, in Section 46, the courts are empowered to pronounce on the constitutionality of any state action and to enforce fundamental rights by making appropriate orders.

Cumulatively, these provisions can be invoked in support of the exercise of judicial review of legislations in Nigeria. Indeed, a plethora of cases exist depicting the utility of the doctrine in Nigerian Courts. See generally: ATTORNEY GENERAL BENDEL v. ATTORNEY GENERAL FEDERATION;[5] WILLIAMS v. MAJEKODUNMI;[6] ADAMOLEKUN v. COUNCIL OF UNIVERSITY OF

[5] *Supra*
[6] (1962) All NLR 413

IBADAN[7] and OLAWOYIN v. COMMISSIONER OF POLICE[8]

STATUTORY EXCLUSION OF JUDICIAL REVIEW

It has now become a fashionable exercise for the legislature to limit the control of the courts in reviewing legislative activities. This is usually done by what is known in constitutional law as ouster clauses. Commendably the judiciary has been unwilling to succumb to these provisions ousting its jurisdiction. Their attitude to these ouster clauses can be gleaned from different cases.

Before the Military intervention in January 1966, the constitution was supreme law of the land. Provisions of ouster clauses were then construed as being contrary to the constitution. For example, in DOHERTY v. BALEWA,[9] the Nigerian parliament unwillingly passed the Tribunals of Enquiry Act, 1961 providing that nothing done by the Prime Minister or the Tribunal in the exercise of their power under the said Act, shall be enquired into by the court of law. This piece of legislation was a direct challenge to the provision of the Independence Constitution. One of those affected by the activities of the tribunal successfully challenged in court, the powers of the Prime Minister under the said Act.

This erstwhile position changed with the coming of the Army in January 1966. During military interregnums, deliberate provisions are inserted in Decrees and Edicts ousting the jurisdiction of courts, since such decrees are perceived as supreme. Two schools exist with regard to the

---

[7] (1967) NMLR 87
[8] 2 All NLR 203
[9] (1961) All NLR 604

judicial attitudes towards ouster clauses. In the first school are those who accept the absoluteness of military decrees and feel helpless. The second school consists of those who believe that in spite of ouster clauses, the courts still have a corrective role to play. Those belonging to the second school do not outwardly question the validity of military legislation but rather, surreptitiously challenge any action done under such legislation that is not in accordance with it.

It would be appropriate to now examine a few cases depicting these judicial attitudes.

(a) Cases showing those who accept absoluteness, of decrees

i) EYO v. CHIEF OF STAFF,[10] the applicant had been ordered to be detained upon a detention order issued under the decree by the respondent. The court came to the conclusion, inter alia, that the detention order could be validly impeached on the ground of uncertainty but, however, proceeded that its jurisdiction was ousted by section 1(2)(b) of the Supremacy and Enforcement of Powers Decree 8 of 1970. The Court in the case ruled that the combined effect of the provisions of Decree No. 2 and No. 13 of 1984 is that on the question of civil liberties, the law courts must as of now, blow muted trumpets.

ii) WANG CHIN YAO & ORS v. CHIEF OF STAFF[11] (SUPREME HEADQUARTERS).

iii) GANI FAWEHINMI v. I.G.P:[12] the applicant was detained on the authority of a detention order which specified, *inter*

---

[10] Case M/130/70 (1970)

[11] (Supreme Headquarters)

[12] (2000) JELR 56914 (CA)

alia, that he had recently been involved in acts prejudicial to state security. The order failed to indicate that it was necessary to exercise control over the applicant by reason of the alleged act.

The learned judge found that the detaining authority had not scrupulously complied with the requirements of Section 1 of Decree No. 2 of 1984. Nevertheless, he held that he was precluded by the decree from adjudicating on the matter.

iv) KOMOLAFE v. ATTORNEY GENERAL FEDERATION The Federal High Court held that if in the opinion of the detaining authority that a person has recently been concerned with acts prejudicial to state security, he cannot be subjected to any scrutiny by the court because the detaining authority is the sole determinant and the degree of certitude cannot be questioned.

(b) Cases showing that courts still have a corrective role to play

i. ADAMOLEKUN v. GOVERNING COUNCIL OF UNIVERSITY OF IBADAN:[13] the question posed before the Supreme Court in this case was whether the court had jurisdiction to look or question the authority of Decree No. 1 of 1966. The court held that it would be nugatory on the powers of the court not to be able to question the validity of an edict vis-à-vis the promulgation of the decree of the Military Government. The court also held that they could enquire into the provisions of any edict so as to ascertain

---

[13] *Supra*

that such provisions were in line with the Federal Government decree.

ii. TUNJI v. FEDERAL COMMISSIONER FOR ESTABLISHMENT,[14] the plaintiff issued a summons for declaration in court that the exercise by the respondent of his discretionary powers under the pensions regulation was null and void. It was found as a fact that the respondent had taken extraneous matters into consideration. The Supreme Court held that the powers of the court to review an exercise of discretion remains intact even when the repository of the discretionary power had not given any reasons for the manner in which his discretion was exercised.

iii. STITCH v. ATTORNEY-GENERAL FEDERATION & ORS,[15] the plaintiff challenged the refusal of the Minister of Commerce to issue her with an import licences for her vehicle imported from West Germany. The Supreme Court held that notwithstanding Section 3(2) of the Finance Act 1981, the Court may in appropriate circumstances infer that the respondent had no good reason for his decision especially if he was influenced by extraneous considerations.

iv. MIKE OZEKHOME & 23 ORS v PRESIDENT,[16] the 1st plaintiff acting on behalf of the others detained under Decree No. 2 of 1984, issued a summons for declaration that the applicants cannot be beheld under the decree. The

[15] (1986) NSCC, p.1389

[16] Unreported

court held that where a detaining authority fails to comply with some conditions precedent in the decree, he goes outside his discretion and to do so would to ultra-vires.

INDEPENDENCE OF JUDICIARY

The importance of maintaining justice is considered fundamental in practically all jurisdictions in the civilized world. This no doubt prompted Schwartz a leading scholar on this subject to remark thus:

> The quality of justice depends more upon the quality of those who administer the law than on the content of the law they administer. Unless those appointed to the bench are competent and upright and are free to judge without fear or favour a judicial system no matter how sound its structure may be on paper, is bound to perform badly in practice.

The phrase "independence" simply connotes that the courts in the discharge of their constitutional functions should not be amenable to the control, interference or direction of the other departments of government. If the courts are afraid of any other department of government, then they can no longer interpret the constitutional impartiality and objectivity in accordance with law.

Independence of the judiciary must never be construed as suggesting that there should be no checks on the courts. Indeed, as a necessity, in order to keep the judge also within the bounds of their powers, the 1999 Constitution provides adequate checks and balances.

Constitutional Measures Guaranteeing An Independent Judiciary

The extent to which the 1999 Constitution has tried to make the judiciary independent can be gleaned from the angle of appointment, conditions of service, tenure of office, removal from office and immunities/privileges.

(i) Appointment

Under the 1999 Constitution, the appointment of the judges of Superior Courts is vested in different bodies. In the case of the Chief Justice of Nigeria, Section 231 provides that he is to be appointed by the President on the recommendation of the National Judicial Council subject to Senatorial confirmation. The candidate is constitutionally required to have fifteen years minimum post-call experience. The other Judges of the Supreme Court, as well as the President of the Court of Appeal are appointed by the President on the recommendation of the National Judicial Council as spelt out in Section 231(2) and 238(1) of the Constitution respectively.

The other judges of the Court of Appeal and Federal High Court are appointed by the President also on the advice of the National Judicial Council. See section 238(2), 249(1) and (2) respectively.

In the state, the Chief Judge, the Grand Khadi and the President of the Customary Court of Appeal are appointed by the Governor on the recommendation of the National Judiciary Council Subject to the approval of the House of Assembly. Other Judges are appointed by the Governor on the recommendation of the National Judiciary Council. See generally section 270, 275 and 280 of the 1999 Constitution.

It can be seen that the Constitution whilst conferring on the Executive the power to appoint judges, has provided checks under that power by requiring confirmation in certain cases and the advice of the National Judicial Council. This is intended to make the judiciary independent and to see that only competent persons are appointed as judges.

(ii) Tenure of office

Once appointed, judges continue to serve up to the age of 65 years with an option to retire at the age of 60 years. A judge who retires after serving in that capacity for not less than 15 years is entitled to pension for life at a rate equivalent to his last annual salary in addition to any other retirement benefits to which he may be entitled.

Where a judge retires at 65 years with less than 15 years of service, he is entitled to pension for life at a rate pro-rata the number of years of service he rendered or to the pension and other retirement benefit to which he is entitled under his terms and conditions of service if any, whichever is higher. See generally Section 291 of the Constitution.

(iii) Remuneration/Conditions of Service

The salaries of judges are charged on the consolidated revenue fund of the Federation. Even though their salaries are determined by the legislature, they cannot be so altered to the prejudice of the judge after appointment. See generally Sections 84 and 124 of the Constitution.

(iv) Removal

Judges can be removed on three grounds spelt out in section 292 (1) of the Constitution: These are:

(a) for inability to perform their functions;
(b) for misconduct; and
(c) for violating the Code of Conduct.

The Chief Executive may remove the Chief Justice of the Federation or the Chief Judge of a state upon the address of the legislature and in other cases, on the recommendation of the Judicial Service Commission. The removal must, however, satisfy the requirement of natural justice. That is to say that the judge concerned should be given adequate hearing and opportunity to make representation against the charges. The case of KALU ANYAH v. ATTORNEY-GENERAL BORNU STATE[17] emphasis that the removal of a judge on any of the three grounds is subject to judicial review by the courts. This therefore serves as sufficient safeguard against arbitrary removal of the judges.

The interposition of the legislature as well as the Judicial Service Commission is again intended, to provide a check on the misuse of the power of removal by the executive. From the foregoing, it would appear that the independence of the judiciary depends, to a large extent, upon the respective Judicial Service Commissions.

The composition of the Federal Judicial Service Commission under the 1999 Constitution is such that it could really function independently without succumbing to the influences of the executive. The Chief Justice, the President of the Court of Appeal and two lawyers from a list of four submitted by the Nigeria Bar Association, and the Attorney-General constitute a majority and could collectively have their

---

[17] 3 NCLR 401

say in matters of appointment and removal. See part one (1) of the 3rd Schedule for the 1999 Constitution.

(v) Immunities/Privileges

Judges of Superior Courts of record in the discharge of their judicial functions are protected from civil liability. They cannot be sued in any court for any act done or order made in the discharge of judicial duties whether or not within the limit of judicial jurisdiction provided that he acted at the time in good faith.

This immunity is not prescribed specifically in the constitution but derives from the various High Court laws. See for example Section 68 High Court Law of Western Region of Nigeria Cap. 44. See also BOYO v. ATAKE[18]

REFERENCES AND FURTHER READING

Chand, H. (1981), *Nigerian Constitution*, Santosh Publishing House, New Delhi.

Nwabueze, B. O (1982), *A Constitutional History of Nigeria*, Longman

Ojo, A. 1987), *Constitutional Law and Military Rule in Nigeria*, Evans Brothers

Oluyede P. A. 0. (1992), *Constitutional Law in Nigeria*, Evans Brothers

Dicey, A.V. (1985), *Introduction to the Study of the Laws of the Constitution*, 10th edition

[18] (1971) I.U.I.L.R. 403

Chapter 9

LEGAL CONSEQUENCES OF CHANGE OF GOVERNMENT BY EXTRA-CONSTITUTIONAL MEANS (*Coup D'état*)

A coup d'état if successful is a revolution – an abrupt change of government not within the contemplation of the constitution. The *Oxford English Dictionary* defines a revolution as an overthrow of an established government by those who were previously subject to it or a forcible substitution of a new ruler or form of government.

Where there is a change of which involves the overthrow of the constitution itself does it also destroy the entire legal order? Does it also destroy the existing state and create a new one?

A German Legal Philosopher Hans Kelsen made the best attempt to explain the nature and effect of revolution when he remarked thus:

> A revolution occurs whenever the legal order of the community is nullified and replaced by a new order in an illegitimate way ... No jurist would maintain that even after a successful revolution, the old constitution and the laws based thereon remain in force on the ground that

> they have not been nullified in a manner anticipated by the old order itself. Every jurist will presume that the old order – to which no political reality any longer corresponds – has ceased to exist.

Kelsen made two distinctions: one is that when a revolution occurs, there are some consequences which naturally flow from such changes and, secondly, that those changes which occur as a result of the deliberate action of the leader of the revolution which may involve changes affecting those that will naturally flow.

The important question is: How far does Kelsen's view about the natural consequences actually represent the position of the law? This can best be answered by citing concrete examples from Ghana, Pakistan and Nigeria.

The question came before the Court of Appeal of Ghana in 1970 in the case of SALLAH v. ATT. GENERAL. In 1966 the Armed forces of Ghana overthrew the government of Kwame Nkrumah. The new government issued a proclamation titled: "A proclamation of the constitution of a National Liberation Council for the Administration of Ghana and for other matters connected therewith." The proclamation inter-alia created the National liberation council as the new authority for Ghana with powers to legislate by Decree. It suspended the 1960 Constitution, dismissed the President and council of ministers, dissolved the National Assembly and proscribed the Convention People Party (CPP).

The proclamation also provided that subject to any Decree any enactment or rule of law in force in Ghana before, the coup shall continue in force but that any such enactment or rule of law can be revoked, repealed or suspended by the Decree.

In 1969, the Armed Forces terminated their rule and returned the country to civilian rule under a new constitution. Among the transitional provisions in the new constitution was one to the effect that every person who before the coming into force of the constitution, held or was acting in any office established during the military regime shall be deemed to have been appointed or to have held office under the constitution of a period of six months from the date of commencement of the constitution.

The plaintiff had been appointed in 1967 as the General Manager of a parastatal. He was dismissed by the new civilian government under the transitional provisions. He brought action challenging the validity of his dismissal. It was argued for the government that the event of 1966 was a coup d'état which abolished all legal order and established a new one in its place and that the effect of this was to destroy the basic law of that order – the constitution. The Attorney General relied on Kelsen's theory which the Court of Appeal rejected.

The court explained the reason for this rejection by saying that "… experience of the world teaches one that there is often considerable diversions between theory and process of authorship and judicial adjudication …"

What the court said in essence was that a coup d'état does not possess any quality of change in itself – it does not change the pre-existing legal order.

The court further held that what happened in Ghana in February, 1966 was just the beginning of the revolution which culminated in the promulgation of the 1969

Constitution which allowed or revoked the 1960 Constitution.

The Supreme Court of Pakistan approved Kelsen's proposition in the case of DOSSO v. STATE when it said:

> A revolution is generally associated with public tumult, mutiny, violence and bloodshed. But from a juristic point of view, the method by which and the persons by whom a revolution is brought about is wholly immaterial...[1]

The court stressed that what is destroyed is not just a constitution but the entire legal order including the public offices and the courts.

The court concluded by saying that a revolution having been successful satisfies the test of efficacy and becomes a basic law creating fact.

This view of the Pakistan Supreme Court was approved by the Supreme Court of Nigeria in LAKANMI v. ATT. GENERAL.[2] This decision came as a shock to the then Federal Military Government which responded by promulgating Decree No. 28 of 1970 to nullify the decision.

The appellants in Lakanmi's case were among other persons whose assets were investigated by the Tribunal of Inquiry set up under an Edict of the Western State Government. The tribunal made an order which restrained the appellant from further dealing with their property except with the approval of the Military Government.

It was this order that the appellant challenged on the ground that it was made in contravention of Section 21 and

---

[1] 1958) 2 PSCR 180

[2] (1971) 1 UILR 201

31 of the 1963 Constitution and that the Edict under which the order was made was invalid in that it was inconsistent with Decree of the Federal Government. Both the High Court and the Court of Appeal did not grant the order sought, but even then the Federal Military Government promulgated three Decrees to aid the respondent. Decree No. 45 was the climax of the efforts in this regard.

The Supreme Court held that Decree No. 45 was invalid and ultra vires the legislative powers of the Federal Military Government. The Court held that Federal Military Government was not a revolutionary government but an interim government necessitated by the event of 1966. It cannot be deemed that the courts are the watch dogs but encroachment into the forbidden zones of the constitution are usually checked by judicial review. But where government has removed the right of courts to review legislative action in certain matters, the courts are bound to respect the provisions of the law especially where the constitution is no longer sovereign. To hold like the Supreme Court held that the legislative competence of the Federal Military Government was ultra vires was to deny the legislative competence of the Federal Military Government and to affirm that the constitution was the Supreme Law of the land; this is not true and the court had no jurisdiction to inquire into the validity of Decree No. 45 of 1968.

The issue in this case are difficult and certainly unprecedented. The decision of the Supreme Court to the effect that the Decree was ultra vires the powers of the Federal Military Government was provision of Section 6 of Decree No. 1 of 1966 and S. 2 of Decree No. 45, of 1968.

The events of January 1966 was a military revolution which had changed the existing legal order and any law including the unaffected parts of the constitution was operative only because the Federal Military Government had adopted it as part of its law.

The legislative power of the Federal Military Government was supreme and could legislate within the limits of physical possibilities on any matter whatsoever.

All that is said above is also true of every military government in Nigeria. For example, when decree No. 1 of 1984 was enacted by the Federal Military Government, it created Supreme Military Council and then the Armed Forces Ruling Council. The Federal Executive Council and the National Council of State which are responsible for the administration of the country at the federal level. While at the state level the state governments subjects to the provision of S.2(2) of Decree No. 1, 1984 are made to be the legislatures assisted by the State Executive Councils in their administration.

The Federal Military gave itself a new legislative power distinct from what the civilian government possessed under the 1979 Constitution. The Federal Military Government could promulgate any decree on any subject in the interest of peace order and good government throughout the country. The combined effect of all these factors is a demonstration of the change of the old legal order. Thus, the former "grundnorm" was deprived of its validity by revolution.

REFERENCES AND FURTHER READING

Aihe D. O. & Oluyede, P. A. O. (1979), *Cases and materials on Constitutional Law*, Ibadan Press.

Ojo, A. (1987), *Constitutional Law & Military Rule in Nigeria,* Evans Brothers

Oluyede P. A. O. (1992*),* *Constitutional Law in Nigeria*, Evans Brothers

Chapter 10

PROCEEDINGS BY AND AGAINST THE STATE

The concept of sovereign immunity is a relic of British jurisprudence. The King at the apex of the federal pyramid was not amenable in what were then 'his court'. Hence the aphorism that the King can do no wrong. The immunity of the sovereign from suits was well recognized and entrenched in the British system. The King could only be sued where he consents.

The virtue of the 1860 Petition of Rights Act, contractual liability on the part of the crown could only be enforced by means of a petition of rights. The present position has changed considerably by the provisions of the Crown Proceedings Act. Contractual liability on the part of the crown can now be enforced by ordinary court processes. The crown however retains immunity in England for tortious liability in respect of acts committed by postal authority, armed forces or judicial officers.

PETITION OF RIGHTS

The procedure has been abolished in England by virtue of the Crown Proceedings Act of 1947. The Act allowed actions of suits be commenced against the government by the ordinary court processes.

In Nigeria however, suits against the government has to be commenced in conformity with the Petition of Right Act 1958 as amended in 1964. The Act provided that all actions against the government may only be commenced with the consent of the Federal Attorney-General or any such person as he may designate as a defendant for that purpose. (See Section 3 of the Petition Rights Act). Commendably, the procedure no longer applies by virtue of the 1979 Constitution (See Section 6(6) of the 1979 Constitution).

The Petition of Rights Act applied hitherto throughout the federation in line with Section 9 thereof. States comprising the former Western and Mid-Western Regions were however excluded. These states had passed their own petition of rights law which were substantially identical to the Federal Act. In ARE v. ATTORNEY-GENERAL of WESTERN REGION[1] the plaintiff successfully claimed compensation for land acquired by the regional government some twenty years previously. The action was commenced by the petition of right. It was alleged by the government that the petition was statute barred. The Appeal Court therefore remitted the action to the High Court for trial on the merit.

Also in the case of LAHAN v. ATTORNEY GENERAL WESTERN REGION[2] the plaintiff similarly commenced an action by filing the petition of right to claim compensation for land acquired by the government. The claim however failed on the ground of having been caught by the statute of limitation. Both cases illustrate the proprietary of commencing action against the government by way of petition of rights.

---

[1] (1960) WNLR 108
[2] (1962) WNLR 319

An important issue raised in relation to a petition of right is the question of which bodies/person could be properly required as a state government functionary so as to warrant the commencement of action against them by filing of the petition of rights. This question came up for determination in the case of ROBERTS v. SULE KATAGUM.[3] Katagum sued the Police Service Commission represented by Robert for unlawfully retiring him from service. The Police Service Commission in its defence claimed to be a state department and as such any suit against it should to be commenced by petition of rights. Taylor C.J. held that the amended petition of rights does not apply in this case. The Police Service Commission cannot claim to be a government of the federation or indeed a ministry or department of a ministry.

By implication therefore only the government ministries and department of ministries are covered within the ambit of the Petition of Rights. It is doubtful whether Justice Taylor's distinction is valid since the Police Service Commission being a government oriented body can be brought within the application of the Petition of Rights Act. However, this decision is consistent with a latter decision in the case of SHITTA-BEY v. FEDERAL PUBLIC SERVICE COMMISSION.[4] In this case, the applicant applied for an order of Mandamus to compel the Federal Public Service Commission to reinstate the applicant who was a former legal adviser to the defendant body. It was contended that the action was not maintainable in law because the Attorney General was not joined as a party. Dismissing the objection the learned trial judge held that the Commission was neither a

[3] Suit No LD/137/65
[4] (1981) ISC 40

government, a government ministry nor department of a ministry such as to bring the case within the Petition of Rights Act.

It would appear that the Petition of Rights Act is not applicable in a suit pertaining to constitutional matters for example in GOVERNOR OF BENDEL STATE v. OBAYUWANA[5] the appointment of the plaintiff as a Customary Court member was cancelled by the Governor of Bendel State under the Customary Court Edict of 1978. The plaintiff challenged the court order as being unconstitutional on the ground that the Customary Court law conflicted with Section 6(4)(a) of the Constitution as is therefore void. The Governor argued that the plaintiff's action was subject to procedural laws of the Petition of Rights Law of Bendel State. The Court of Appeal held that the citizen has a right to seek any redress in court for the determination of any question as to the civil rights and obligations of the person. Therefore, where the declarative action raises a constitutionalism it cannot be inhibited by procedural laws such as the petition of rights law and the public officer protection law. This decision clearly illustrates that the form in which an action is formulated may determine its outcome. By invoking the principle of natural justice the Obayuwana's case takes the issue in dispute out of the realm of breach of contract.

It should be noted however that since the promulgation of the 1979 Constitution the doctrine of state immunity and all procedural laws deriving therefrom have ceased to apply in Nigeria. This is clearly borne out in the case of RANSOME KUTI v. ATTORNEY GENERAL OF THE FEDERATION.[6]

---

[5] (1982) 3 NCLR 206
[6] (1985) 6 SC 246

The appellant in that case sued the Federal Government claiming the sum of ₦25,000,000 for the burning down of his property by soldiers, the court held that the plaintiff's case was founded upon tort and the common law of state immunity being applicable in Nigeria in 1977 when the cause of action arose, the state cannot be made liable for the tortious act of its servant or agent. It was further held that although the common law of state principle for tortious act has been abolished in England by virtue of Section 2 of the Crown Proceedings Act of 1947, this is not so in Nigeria because the Act does not apply in Nigeria. On the contrary, the Petition of Rights Act as amended in 1964 has further given the stamp of authority to the Common Law principle in Nigeria. It was further held that Section 6(6) of the 1979 Constitution which vested judicial power of the state on the court has removed and abolished the common law doctrine of state immunity from tortious liability in Nigeria. (See GOVERNOR OF IMO STATE v. GRECCO CONSTRUCTION and ENGINEERING ASSOCIATION LTD)[7]

PROTECTION OF PUBLIC OFFICERS AGAINST TORTIOUS LIABILITY

Another ambit of the concept of sovereign immunity is the protection given to public officers in respect of actions founded upon tortious conducts. The *locus classicus* on this issue in Nigeria is the case of FASORO v. MILBORNE & OTHERS.[8] The plaintiff in this case sued the defendant an Assistant District Officer for assault and battery. The defendant had instructed a police man attached to him to

[7] (1985) 3 NWLR PART 11 PAGE 71
[8] (1923) 4 NLR 85

strike the plaintiff in the course of conducting a provincial court. While holding the A.D.O as a public officer for the purposes of this case, the court however noted that the action of the A.D.O was unlawful in that it was not necessary for the execution of his duty. He was therefore held liable for damages in assault.

In OBIEFUNA v. OKOYE[9] the plaintiff was informed when a vehicle being driven by the defendant a police constable collided with him. He brought an action for damages against the police constable it was argued for the defendant that being a public officer an action against him could only commence within a statutory period of three (3) months, the court upheld the contention of the defendant and dismissed the plaintiff's action. The issue of what category of person fall within the definition of "public officer" has being a subject of varying judicial interpretation. The decision in OBIEFUNA v. OKOYE and FASORO v. MILBORNE shows that a constable and an A.D.O respectively are public officers so as to bring them within the protection of the Act.

Similarly EKEMODE v. ALAUSA[10] in this case, a road over seer working for the Epe District Council destroyed the plaintiff's canoe in pursuance of a directive of the Council that the water way and the landing route at Epe waterside should be cleared. The plaintiff thereupon sued the defendant for damages. The defendant contended that the action was statute barred having being commenced 3 months after the event and bearing in mind that he was a public officer who was entitle to claim the protection under the Act. In the view of the court the provision of the Act which refers to "any person acting in

---

[9] (1961) All NLR 357
[10] (1961) All NLR 135

execution of a public duty" was wide enough to cover persons whose employment required them to act pursuant to or in execution of or intended execution of any ordinance or any public duty or authority whatever his grade.

It follows from the above decision that ministers, commissioners, heads of departments, heads of corporations or local authority, quasi-government institutions, their subordinate staff and also members of the armed forces and the police are within the protection of the Act. The test use is on function and authority. However, this wide definition of public officer did not seem to have found favour in MOMOH v. OKEWALE[11] in this case, a driver of Lagos City Council and the Council were sued for negligence by the plaintiff who was injured in an accident involving a vehicle of the Council, the driver claimed that he was a public officer and thereby entitled to protection. The High Court upheld the plea. On appeal to the Supreme Court however, it was held that the driver of the Lagos City Council could not be a public officer, the decision in Momoh's case appears rather unduly restrictive since it would mean that persons engaged in quasi-government institutions would lose protection of the Act.

Under Section 7 of the Public Officers (Special Provisions) Decree No. 10 of 1976 a public officer is defined now as "a person holding office in the service of a body whether corporate or incorporate established under a federal or state law" this law extends the definition of public officers to persons holding offices in a company in which any of the government of Nigeria has a controlling or substantial interest.

---

[11] (1977) 6 SC 81

Aside from the definition of public officers provided in the cases already mentioned under this heading, the same cases also illustrates that the public officer is protected only in so far as he acts lawfully in pursuant of his functions or duties. For example, in Fasoro's case the A.D.O was held liable for assault because the act was not incidental to the execution of his duty as A.D.O. In Obiefuna's case while holding that the limitation of or protection in point of time for commencement of action against the police constable was absolute nevertheless awarded damages against the defendant. In Ekemode's case the court held that even though the overseer was a public officer he had acted unlawfully and beyond his mandate by wilfully destroying the plaintiff's canoe in execution of a directive "to clear the waterway and landing routes."

From the foregoing we can summarize that sovereign immunity is an English doctrine of great antiquity originating from the old feudalist structure of the old English society. The basis of the doctrine is that the King can do no wrong. This old English doctrine was imported into Nigeria by the old colonial masters' administration. Although the doctrine has witnessed drastic in the country of origin it remained a part of Nigerian law until the coming into effect of the 1979 Constitution.

REFERENCES FOR FURTHER READING

Nwabueze B.O., *Military Rule and Constitutionalism*

Ojo, J. D., *The Development of the Executive under the Nigerian Constitutions* (1960-1981)

Ojo, A (1987), *Constitutional Law and Military Rule in Nigeria*, Evans Brothers.

Shyllon, F. & Obasanjo, O., *The Demise of the Rule of Law in Nigeria under the Military*. Two points of view.

INDEX

I

J

K

L

www.ingramcontent.com/pod-product-compliance
Lightning Source LLC
Chambersburg PA
CBHW050528240926
51846CB00003B/732
9789786061887